Industrial Relations in Fleet Street

Warwick Studies in Industrial Relations

General Editors: G. S. Bain and H. A. Clegg

Industrial Relations in Fleet Street

A STUDY IN PAY STRUCTURE

Keith Sisson

BASIL BLACKWELL · OXFORD

0 631 16530 4

Printed in Great Britain by
Compton Printing Ltd
Aylesbury

Contents

Pay Structure; Manning Levels and Working
Practices; Machinery for Change

APPENDICES

Editors' Foreword

Warwick University's first undergraduates were admitted in 1965. The teaching of industrial relations began a year later, and in 1967 a one-year graduate course leading to an MA in Industrial Relations was introduced. Research in industrial relations also commenced in 1967 with a grant from the Clarkson Trustees, and in 1970 received a major impetus when the Social Science Research Council established its Industrial Relations Research Unit at Warwick.

The series of Warwick Studies in Industrial Relations was launched in 1972 as the main vehicle for the publication of the results of the Unit's projects. It is also intended to include the research carried out by staff teaching industrial relations in the University and, where it merits publication, the work of graduate students. The first six titles in the series were published by Heinemann Educational Books, but publication has now been transferred to Basil Blackwell and Mott.

Keith Sisson is a lecturer in industrial relations in the School of Industrial and Business Studies at Warwick and an Associate Fellow of the Industrial Relations Research Unit. Before coming to Warwick, he was Labour Secretary of the Newspaper Publishers Association, which covers the Fleet Street papers. His study starts from the exceptionally full and detailed statistics of earnings in Fleet Street which were available to him for the period 1961-70. They enable him to give a more precise account of the pay structure there than is available for most other industries. But in seeking to explain this structure he also examines many of the characteristics which are now popularly associated with Fleet Street industrial relations, as well as the variables believed by labour economists to determine pay structures. This analysis focuses on the development of a system of 'payment by task' and the 'pattern bargaining' which takes place between management and union 'chapels'. His main conclusion is that the key to most aspects of industrial relations in Fleet Street lies in the reaction of managers and chapels to the product market.

The peculiarities of Fleet Street have long held a fascination for students of industrial relations; but the desperate economic situation of several national newspapers is a matter of widespread concern. Keith Sisson's study sheds light both on a number of issues of central interest to industrial relations specialists and labour economists, and on an important aspect of newspaper economics.

George Bain

Hugh Clegg

List of Tables

List of Abbreviations

ACP   Association of Correctors of the Press (amalgamated with NGA, 1966)

ASLP   Amalgamated Society of Lithographic Printers (amalgamated with NGA, 1969)

AUEW   Amalgamated Union of Engineering Workers (formerly Amalgamated Union of Engineering and Foundry Workers and Amalgamated Engineering Union)

BFMP   British Federation of Master Printers

CIR   Commission on Industrial Relations

EIU   Economist Intelligence Unit

EEPTU Electrical, Electronic, and Plumbing Trade Union (formerly Electrical, Electronic Telecommunications Union/Plumbing Trades Union, and Electrical Trades Union)

FOC   Father of Chapel

IPC   International Publishing Corporation (subsidiary of Reed International Ltd and publishers of *Daily* and *Sunday Mirror*, (Sunday) *People*, and *Sporting Life*)

LCB   London Central Branch of SOGAT (formerly NUPB & PW)

LMPA   London Master Printers' Association

LSC   London Society of Compositors (amalgamated with PMMTS in 1955 to form LTS)

LTS   London Typographical Society (amalgamation of LSC and PMMTS, 1955. Amalgamated with TA in1964 to form NGA)

NATSOPA	National Society of Operative Printers, Graphical and Media Personnel (formerly National Society of Operative Printers and Assistants)
NBPI	National Board for Prices and Incomes
NGA	National Graphical Association (amalgamation of LTS and TA in 1964)
NPA	Newspaper Publishers Association (formerly Newspaper Proprietors Association)
NSES	National Society of Electrotypers and Stereotypers (amalgamated with NGA, 1967)
NUJ	National Union of Journalists
NUPB & PW	National Union of Printing, Bookbinding and Paper Workers (subsequently SOGAT)
NUPT	National Union of Press Telegraphists (amalgamated with NGA, 1966)
PKTF	Printing and Kindred Trades' Federation
PMB	Printing Machine Branch of SOGAT (formerly NUPB & PW)
PMMTS	Printing Machine Managers' Trade Society (amalgamated with LSC in 1955 to form LTS)
RIRMA	Revisers, Ink and Roller Makers, and Auxiliaries Branch of NATSOPA
SDNS	Scottish Daily Newspaper Society
SLADE	Society of Lithographic Artists, Designers, Engravers and Process Workers
SNPA	Scottish Newspaper Proprietors' Association
SOGAT	Society of Graphical and Allied Trades (amalgamation of NATSOPA, Division 1, and NUPB & PW, Division A, 1966. Title subsequently adopted by Division A)
TA	Typographical Association (amalgamated with LTS in 1964 to form NGA)
TUC	Trades Union Congress

NB   As far as possible current titles are used in the text.

Chapter 1

Introduction

This is a study of industrial relations in Fleet Street. As such, there is hardly any need to justify its undertaking. Fleet Street, like the docks and the car industry, has long had a fascination for the student of industrial relations. Some of the reasons which help to account for this interest are well known. The NBPI, for example, confirmed that 'earnings are very much higher than in manufacturing industry generally, averaging in 1968 (the last year for which figures are available) approximately £48 per week for craft workers, and £42 per week for non-craft workers'.[1] The NBPI also reminded its readers that 'the Royal Commission Report on the Press of 1962 and the Economist Intelligence Unit's Report revealed gross inefficiencies in the production of national newspapers, mainly due to over-manning'.[2] Another interesting characteristic is the structure of collective bargaining. As well as negotiations between the NPA and the trade unions, there is also the 'highly developed system of chapel bargaining'.[3]

But these and other characteristics can be regarded in a different light — it is often suggested that they are a major contributory factor in the desperate economic situation of many national newspapers. The decision of Beaverbrook Newspapers Ltd in March 1974 to close the *Glasgow Evening Citizen* and to transfer printing of the *Scottish*

1. NBPI Report No. 141, *Costs and Revenue of National Newspapers*, Cmnd. 4277 (London: HMSO, 1969), p. 13.
2. *ibid.*, p. 13.
   The references are to the *Report of the Royal Commission on the Press*, Cmnd. 1811 (London: HMSO, 1962), and the Report of the Economist Intelligence Unit, *The National Newspaper Industry: A Survey*, 1967. Both reports give estimates of the over-manning.
3. H. A. Clegg, *The System of Industrial Relations in Great Britain* (Oxford: Blackwell, 1970), p. 275. See also W. E. J. McCarthy, *The Role of Shop Stewards in British Industrial Relations*, Royal Commission Research Paper No. 1 (London: HMSO, 1967), p. 48.

Daily Express and *Scottish Sunday Express* to Manchester, coupled with reports that the group as a whole is in difficulties, has once again raised questions about the future financial viability of a number of the newspapers. As a result, the Labour Government has announced the setting up of the third Royal Commission on the Press in less than thirty years.[4]

Aims and Method

The study which follows attempts to explain the main features of the pay structure or *relative levels of pay*[5] of production and maintenance workers in ten of the newspaper offices listed in Table 1.1. In each case the newspaper office is situated in or near Fleet Street.[6] Of those listed, the so-called 'Sunday only' offices, i.e. *News of the World, Observer, Sunday People* and the *Sunday Times*, have not been included on account of the very different patterns of working.[7] The other office not included is the *Sun*, since in this case the changes in ownership made it virtually impossible to give a continuous picture of the pay structure.

Details of the occupations in the production and maintenance departments will be found in the third section of this chapter. In view of recent developments in industrial relations, the decision not

4. The first Royal Commission on the Press was set up in 1947 and reported in 1949. The second was set up in 1961 and reported in 1962.
5. This is the simple definition of pay structure. Later the study distinguishes the inter-office pay structure, or relative levels of pay between the different newspaper offices, and the internal pay structures or relative levels of pay within each office. See, for example, W. M. Conboy and D. Robinson, 'Wages Structures and Internal Labour Markets' in D. Robinson (ed.), *Local Labour Markets and Wage Structures* (London: Gower, 1970), p. 215. See also J. T. Dunlop, 'The Task of Contemporary Wage Theory', in F. E. Pierson and G. W. Taylor (eds.), *New Concepts in Wage Determination* (New York: McGraw Hill, 1957) and G. H. Hildebrand, 'External Influences and the Determination of Internal Wage Structure', in J. L. Meij (ed.), *Internal Wage-Structure* (Amsterdam: North Holland, 1963).
6. The following newspapers also printed their northern editions in Manchester in 1970: the *Daily Mirror* and *Sunday Mirror*, the *Daily Express* and *Sunday Express*, the *Daily Telegraph* and *Sunday Telegraph*, the *Daily Mail*, the *Guardian*, the *Sunday People*, and the *News of the World*.
7. For example, the bulk of the labour force in the machine and publishing departments is required on Saturday only. Occupations in the other production departments usually work four days a week, Saturday being a double shift.

TABLE 1.1

NATIONAL NEWSPAPERS IN MEMBERSHIP OF NPA (1970)

Newspaper	Company
Daily Mail *Evening News* *Daily Sketch*	Associated Newspapers Group Ltd
* *Daily Express* * *Sunday Express* *Evening Standard*	Beaverbrook Newspapers Ltd
Daily Mirror * *Sunday Mirror* (1963)[a] *People*[b]	Reed International Ltd
* *Daily Telegraph* * *Sunday Telegraph* (1961)[c]	Daily Telegraph Ltd
Financial Times	Pearson Longman Ltd
Guardian (1963)[d]	Manchester Guardian and Evening News Ltd
The Times (1966)[e] *Sunday Times*	Thomson Organization Ltd
Sun (1969)[f] *News of the World*	News International Ltd
Observer	Observer (Holdings) Ltd

NOTES

*   'Dual' office in which daily and Sunday newspapers are published

a   Title changed from *Sunday Pictorial*

b   Title subsequently changed to *Sunday People*

c   *Sunday Telegraph* first published

d   *Guardian* joined NPA

e   *The Times* taken over by Thomson Organization

f   *Sun* (changed from *Daily Herald*, 1964) taken over by News of the World Organization

Other newspapers in membership of NPA were *Sporting Life* (Reed International Ltd) and *Morning Advertiser* (Society of Licensed Victuallers).
News Chronicle and *Star* closed 1960; *Sunday Dispatch* 1961; *Sunday Citizen* (Reynolds News) 1967; *Greyhound Express* 1969.

to include the editorial and clerical departments in the study might be thought surprising.[8] Yet the significance of these developments, many of which were the result of the reaction of journalists and clerical workers to the situation described here, helps to explain why these departments have not been included — it would simply not be possible to do justice to them in the same study.

The study begins in 1961 because this was the first year in which the data were complete. It ends in 1970 for two reasons. Every attempt has been made throughout the study to preserve the identity of the newspapers. If the study had continued beyond 1970, it would not have been possible to preserve the identity of the *Daily Mail* and the *Daily Sketch* which were merged in 1970. Also, it seemed sensible not to include more recent information in case it prejudiced the outcome of negotiations taking place at the time of publication.

The decision to make the pay structure the focus of the study requires some explanation. There seemed little point in following in the footsteps of previous inquiries into Fleet Street[9] which had moved too quickly from description to prescription in their treatment of industrial relations. The fact that nothing seemed to happen despite their exhortations — and despite a great deal of activity in Fleet Street itself — only confirmed that what was needed above all else was adequate explanation. An investigation into the pay structure offered a unique opportunity to attempt this. In particular, it made it possible for the study to consider most, if not all, of the characteristics which have come to be associated with industrial relations in Fleet Street and to relate them to other variables in the wider context of the newspapers. So an approach could be adopted which was essentially analytical rather than historical or descriptive.

A second reason for making the pay structure the focus is that it has been a major source of conflict in Fleet Street. Attempts to negotiate revisions to the industry basic rates led to industrial action on the part of the trade unions or the employers' association in 1968, 1970 and 1971. Significantly, the conflict resulted not from straightforward pay claims but from claims or proposals which threatened to upset traditional differentials both in the industry

8. See, for example, the events described in NBPI Report No. 145, *Journalists' Pay*, Cmnd. 4077 (London: HMSO, 1969). Journalists are organized by the NUJ and clerical and administrative workers by NATSOPA.
9. The reference is to the reports of the Economist Intelligence Unit, the NBPI, and the Royal Commission on the Press, 1961-2.

4

basic rates and in occupational earnings.[10] There have also been disputes over the pay structure in the individual newspaper offices. As a result of one such dispute involving members of the NGA and NATSOPA in the machine department, the *Daily Mirror* and *Sunday Mirror* lost more than ten million copies in 1969 and 1970.[11]

It is also hoped that an investigation into the pay structure will be of intrinsic interest. Very little is known about the ways in which pay structures evolve especially at plant level under conditions of collective bargaining. As recently as 1969 it was stated that there had been 'an almost complete absence of empirical investigation into plant level pay structure in the United Kingdom'.[12] While a number of studies in the engineering industry have helped to fill the vacuum,[13] Fleet Street offers excellent opportunities for further research.

Analytical Framework

The three chapters in Part I of the study describe the main features of the pay structure in the ten newspaper offices. Chapter 2 describes the inter-office pay structure and Chapter 3 the internal pay structures. Chapter 4 has two objectives. One is to describe the large number and variety of the components of pay. The other is to establish the relative significance of differences and changes in the components of pay negotiated by the NPA and the trade unions on the one hand, and the managements and chapels on the other.

The task of analysis is begun in Part II in Chapter 5, which looks

10. Appendices II and III describe the background to these disputes. Of course, Fleet Street has not been unique in its experience. The CIR, for example, had shown pay systems and pay structures to be a major cause of conflict in a number of the companies studied in its reports. Report No. 4 on the Birmid Qualcast subsidiaries is an excellent example. See *First General Report*, CIR Report No. 9, Cmnd. 4417 (London: HMSO, 1970). *Birmingham Aluminium Casting Co. Ltd*, CIR Report No. 4, Cmnd. 4264 (London: HMSO, 1970). For a discussion of the significance of wages in the British strike pattern, see *Report of the Royal Commission on Trade Unions and Employers' Associations*, Cmnd. 3623 (London: HMSO, 1968), ch. 7; and R. Hyman, *Strikes* (London: Fontana, 1972), pp. 117-19.
11. The dispute is described in Appendix I.
12. S. W. Lerner *et al.*, *Workshop Wage Determination* (Oxford: Pergamon, 1969), p. 9.
13. See, in particular, D. I. MacKay *et al.*, *Labour Markets under Different Employment Conditions* (London: Allen and Unwin, 1971), and D. Robinson (ed.), *op. cit.*

at the work situation. The first section of this chapter examines the significance of the location of the newspaper offices. The second tests for relationships between the findings in Chapters 2 and 3 and a number of variables under the heading of the 'technology of production'. The third examines the significance of the patterns of working.

Chapter 6 examines the labour market. The first section of this chapter considers the possibility that the characteristics of the labour force in the different offices will offer an explanation. The second section explains why workers in the production and maintenance departments are unable to respond to differences and changes in the levels of earnings by moving from occupation to occupation and from office to office. The third and fourth sections respectively examine the significance of the employment situation in the printing industry and the decasualization in the machine and publishing departments.

Chapter 7 examines the significance of conditions in the product market. The first section tests for relationships between the findings in Chapters 2 and 3 and the levels of activity in the markets for readers and advertisers — the copy sales and page sizes of the newspapers. The second section examines the significance of the competition with other media. The fourth and final section of this chapter examines the ability to pay of the different newspapers.

The next four chapters are concerned with the parties to industrial relations. The first sections of Chapters 8 and 10 discuss the goals and constraints of the chapels and the managements, while the second sections examine the extent to which the attitudes and policies of these two parties help to explain the findings in Chapters 2, 3 and 4. The first sections of Chapters 9 and 11 attempt to explain why the trade unions and the employers' association were unable to make major changes in the structure of the industry basic rates. The second sections examine the influence of the trade unions and employers' association on negotiations between the chapels and the managements. Chapter 12 presents the main conclusions of the study.

The appendices have been included partly because of the intrinsic interest of the disputes they describe and partly because they help to illustrate the relationships between the parties. Appendix I describes the differential dispute involving members of the NGA and NATSOPA in the machine department of the *Daily Mirror* in 1969 and 1970. Appendix II discusses the SLADE dispute of 1968 and Appendix III the SOGAT dispute in 1970, both of which resulted from the failure of the NPA and the trade unions to agree revisions to the industry basic rates.

The division of Part II as described above is largely dictated by the need to examine systematically not only a number of variables in the context of the newspapers, but also the attitudes and policies of the parties. However, it is inevitably somewhat arbitrary. For instance, Chapter 5 refers to the significance of the discontinuities in production of the newspapers, but this subject could just as well have been discussed in Chapter 7 since these discontinuities are the result of changes in the product and fluctuations in the level of activity in the product market. It must also be emphasized that the objective in Chapters 5, 6 and 7 is to establish whether or not there are significant relationships between the main features of the pay structure and the different variables examined. Later chapters explain more fully the meanings which the parties attach to these relationships. Chapter 7, for example, argues that the ability to pay of the newspapers does not appear to have been significant — at least in the short run. The explanation for this is to be found in Chapters 8 and 10, which discuss the goals and constraints of the chapels and the managements.

The perspective which underpins the framework set out above also must be made explicit. Whereas most recent empirical studies of pay structures have treated the relative levels of pay simply as factor prices,[14] this study treats them as 'another group of rules of the work-place'.[15] Had it not done so, there would have been no place for many of the variables referred to in the framework.[16] But the

14. See, for example, Lerner, *et al., op. cit.*; MacKay *et al., op. cit.*
15. J. T. Dunlop, *Industrial Relations Systems* (reissued, Carbondale: Southern Illinois University Press, 1970), p. 285. It should be emphasized that this perspective is consistent with the view of collective bargaining as essentially a rule-making process which determines many of the norms, procedural as well as substantive, governing behaviour at work. See also N. W. Chamberlain and J. W. Kuhn, *Collective Bargaining*, 2nd edn (New York: McGraw Hill, 1965); Clegg, *op. cit.*; A. Flanders, *Management and Trade Unions* (London: Faber and Faber, 1970); A. Fox, *A Sociology of Work in Industry* (London: Collier-Macmillan, 1971); C. Kerr and A. Siegal, 'Structuring of the Labour Force in Industrial Society', in *Industrial and Labor Relations Review* (Jan. 1955); K. Walker, *Research Needs in Industrial Relations* (Perth: University of Western Australia Press, 1964).
16. The study draws on a number of theoretical frameworks besides Dunlop's for these variables. The main sources are referred to in later notes. A useful

point has a relevance beyond the aims and method of this study. Few, if any, of the studies adopting the traditional perspective have been able to offer more than a partial explanation for those relative levels of pay settled by collective bargaining. The reasons for this might be disputed, but the fact that the traditional perspective restricts analysis to competitive market forces must be regarded as a major consideration. This is not to say that these forces are unimportant. But there is a need to show how they work through the institutions and processes of collective bargaining. Indeed, if this is not done their true significance might be lost.

Naturally, this study is indebted to Dunlop for both its framework and its perspective. However, those who are familiar with Dunlop's work might be surprised to find that there is no other reference to an 'industrial relations system'.[17] The omission is quite deliberate. If the phrase is used to describe a set of variables in some way related to each other, then there can be little quarrel with its use. If, on the other hand, it is used, as it is by Dunlop, to denote a theory of social action, it implies a consensus among the parties which, at the very least, is questionable.[18] Since it would not have been used in this strict sense, and yet might still lead to misunderstanding, it was decided not to use the phrase at all.

How a Newspaper is Made

It only remains in this Introduction to describe how a newspaper is made and to give details of the occupations in the production and maintenance departments. Diagram 1.1 shows the location of the occupations in the manufacturing process.

summary of the literature appears in H. M. Levinson, *Determining Forces in Collective Wage Bargaining* (New York: J. Wiley, 1966).

17. For Dunlop: 'an industrial relations system at any one time in its development is regarded as comprised of certain actors, certain contexts, an ideology which binds the industrial relations system together, and a body of rules created to govern the actors at the work-place and work community.' *op. cit.*, p. 7.

18. For a more detailed discussion of the use of systems theory, see A. N. J. Blain and J. Gennard, 'Industrial Relations Theory: A Critical Review', *British Journal of Industrial Relations* (Nov. 1970); P. S. Cohen, *Modern Social Theory* (London: Heinemann, 1968); J. E. T. Eldridge, *Industrial Disputes* (London: Routledge and Kegan Paul, 1968); J. R. Rex, *Key Problems of Sociological Theory* (London: Routledge and Kegan Paul, 1961); D. Silverman, *The Theory of Organisations* (London: Heinemann, 1970).

DIAGRAM 1.1
LOCATION OF OCCUPATIONS IN THE MANUFACTURING PROCESS

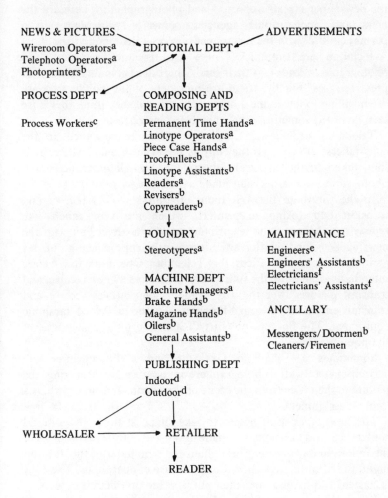

NEWS & PICTURES ⟶ EDITORIAL DEPT ⟵ ADVERTISEMENTS

Wireroom Operators[a]
Telephoto Operators[a]
Photoprinters[b]

PROCESS DEPT ⟵ COMPOSING AND READING DEPTS

Process Workers[c]

Permanent Time Hands[a]
Linotype Operators[a]
Piece Case Hands[a]
Proofpullers[b]
Linotype Assistants[b]
Readers[a]
Revisers[b]
Copyreaders[b]
↓

FOUNDRY

Stereotypers[a]
↓

MACHINE DEPT

Machine Managers[a]
Brake Hands[b]
Magazine Hands[b]
Oilers[b]
General Assistants[b]

PUBLISHING DEPT

Indoor[d]
Outdoor[d]

MAINTENANCE

Engineers[e]
Engineers' Assistants[b]
Electricians[f]
Electricians' Assistants[f]

ANCILLARY

Messengers/Doormen[b]
Cleaners/Firemen

WHOLESALER ⟶ RETAILER

READER

KEY

a   National Graphical Association
b   National Society of Operative Printers, Graphical and Media Personnel
c   Society of Lithographic Artists, Designers, Engravers and Process Workers
d   Society of Graphical and Allied Trades
e   Amalgamated Union of Engineering Workers
f   Electrical, Electronic, and Plumbing Trade Union

News is the life-blood of a newspaper, and there is a continuous flow into a newspaper office from many different sources. There are the newspaper's 'staff' reporters and photographers. There are the news and photographic agencies, some of which provide a permanent link with the newspaper office — Reuters and the Press Association are examples. There are freelance reporters and photographers, known as 'stringers'. There are press statements and press releases. Finally, there are members of the public who are often willing to telephone a newspaper office if they think they have seen or heard something that may be of interest.

Telephone callers with news or stories are re-routed to the copy-takers who type out the copy as the caller speaks. The copy is then taken to the editorial department, like all other news and photographs, and a decision made as to its news value.

In the wireroom the Wireroom Operators (NGA) receive and transmit copy using teleprinters, which are very much like typewriters. Many of the teleprinters provide a direct link with the news agencies and chatter away incessantly, copy pouring out day and night. In some offices the Telephoto Operators (NGA) are interchangeable with the Wireroom Operators. They receive and transmit pictures over the wire, and in some offices receive and transmit entire pages from Manchester, using advanced facsimile equipment. The Photoprinters (NATSOPA) print the negatives of the photographs.

Sometimes a Telephoto Operator and a Photoprinter will accompany a 'staff' photographer on a story, transmitting the picture to the office from the scene of the action. This is known as a 'mobile assignment'.

The newspaper itself begins to take shape at the daily editorial conference, and decisions are made about the outline and themes of the following day's issue. Throughout the remainder of the day and night, the editorial department is the centre of operations. The copy is 'tasted', sub-edited, and then put into the production process.

When the copy leaves the editorial department, it goes to the composing department where it is divided into roughly equal parts at the copy desk. The Linotype Operator (NGA) takes some copy and sets it in lines of hot metal on his linotype machine. He then returns the type and the copy to the random desk where it is placed along-side the type produced by the other Operators. In the meantime, the Piece Case Hand (NGA) produces the large type for head-lines and the rules used to divide the page, hand-setting the characters from existing stock or manufacturing them with the use of a Ludlow or Monotype machine. The Permanent Time Hand or 'Stab' Hand (NGA) makes up the page by taking the type produced by his fellow compositors and inserting it into a forme which is a frame about the size of the page.

The 'make-up' of the page is the critical stage in the manufacturing process. Here the type and the picture blocks come together. The forme in which the page is 'locked up' represents the 'first copy' which is then ready to go into the mass production stage; and the newspapers have set times by which the various pages have to be 'off stone', the name for the table on which the Permanent Time Hand makes up the page.

Two other occupations are involved in the composing department. The Linotype Assistant (NATSOPA) performs a number of ancillary duties: for example, he is responsible for keeping the linotype machines supplied with metal. The Proofpuller (SOGAT) takes a proof of each story or feature as it is completed. These proofs are then returned to the editorial department for changes or to the reading department for checking, this cycle taking place a number of times before everyone is satisfied.

In the reading department the Reader (NGA) checks the proof and the Copy-reader (NATSOPA) the copy. Corrected proofs are then checked for final errors by the Reviser (NATSOPA).

Photographs go to the picture desk in the editorial department where the Picture Editor decides which photographs shall appear in the newspaper. The ones that receive his approval then go to the process department. Here the members of SLADE are engaged in a number of tasks associated with the production of a sensitized metal plate on which the image of the picture appears. In one or two offices proving is done by Process Provers who are members of the PMB of SOGAT.

The Stereotypers (NGA) are involved in three main activities. In the bench room they produce the metal blocks that mount the plates made in the process department; they also rout the blocks from the advertising agencies. In the moulding department, which is usually adjacent to the composing department, they produce a mould of the forme, known as a 'flong', from which the metal plate that eventually is fitted to the cylinders on the rotary presses in the machine department is cast. Sometimes 'foundry' is used to describe the activities in which the Stereotypers are involved.

The next stage in the manufacturing process is the machine department. These tend to be vast, noisy places with lines of rotary presses pouring out thousands of copies each hour of the run. The machine crew consists of the Machine Manager (NGA) and the assistants (NATSOPA). The Machine Manager is responsible for the quality of the copy. The Brake Hand, who is the most senior of the assistants, is responsible for the speed, tension, and braking of the press; he also supervises the 'sheeting' or reloading of the magazine with newsprint. The Oiler is responsible for lubricating the units; he also puts the metal plates on the cylinder, and he helps in the 'sheeting'. The Magazine Hand is responsible for 'dressing' or preparing the newsprint reel. Then there are a number of General Assistants who perform a variety of tasks. The 'Fly-hands', for example, remove the copies from the 'fly', which is the point at which they emerge from the press. Others are responsible for cleaning the presses and the machine department generally. In some offices General Assistants also form the 'day' reel gangs which transport the newsprint reels into the office.

In the publishing department or warehouse the members of SOGAT wrap, label, and dispatch the newspapers. These are then taken by van to the mainline railway terminals by members of the same union or are collected by wholesalers' employees who are also members of SOGAT.

With the exception of the wireroom and telephoto departments, maintenance is carried out by Electricians and their Assistants (EEPTU) and by Engineers (AUEW) and their Assistants who are members of NATSOPA. Messengers, Doormen, Cleaners, and Firemen are also members of NATSOPA.

Part 1
The Pay Structure

Chapter 2

The Inter-office Pay Structure

In presenting the findings in this and the next two chapters a number of steps have been taken to ease the congestion which is an inevitable problem in empirical studies of pay structures. First, the analysis is restricted to the earnings of workers on the shift which is engaged in the production of the newspaper. Otherwise the earnings of some occupations would have had to have been presented in triplicate because there are three separate shifts in each twenty-four-hour cycle. There would also have been problems in dealing with the differences between the daily newspapers which are printed at night and the evening newspapers which are printed during the day. Second, the findings of only four of the years are presented here — 1961, 1964, 1967 and 1970. Besides being equidistant, these years are also the ones in which the data were most complete. Third, the findings are presented in summary form.

It should also be noted that the measure of pay is the gross average weekly earnings of regular[1] workers for the month of October. The source is the annual earnings survey carried out by the NPA. This measure is the most appropriate for the purposes of this study for the same reason that the data is collected in this form by the employers' association. The industry basic rates in themselves are an inadequate measure because of the earnings gap.[2] Other measures such as standard hourly or weekly earnings, which discount overtime and shift pay, have little meaning in Fleet Street because of the difficulties in distinguishing these payments from the

---

1. The situation of casual workers is discussed more fully in Chapter 6. They usually receive the same earnings per shift as regular workers but no details of their number is contained in the NPA's earnings survey.
2. The earnings gap is the difference between the industry basic rates and gross earnings.

many other components of pay.[3] The fact that the earnings are averaged does not present any real problems, since there is little, if any, variation in the earnings of members of the same occupation in each office: the chapel negotiates standard components or rates for all its members. This is even true of the Linotype Operators and Piece Case Hands who are the only ones paid by results. The London Scale of Prices under which they are paid is individually based, i.e. each individual completes a docket showing the amount he has earned, but the earnings in most offices are pooled into what is known as a 'general', and each man takes an equal share.[4]

For all this, the measure of pay used here is not without its deficiencies.[5] Pay weeks may differ from office to office. In the early period of the study, before the negotiation of comprehensive agreements, no month was entirely representative because of the tendency for earnings to fluctuate from week to week. There must be doubts too about accuracy in some cases. But then these are typical of the problems which confront empirical studies of pay structures.

Differences in Earnings between Offices

It might be thought that there would be very little difference in earnings between the offices. But nothing could be further from the truth. Despite their close proximity to one another there were very

3. For a discussion of these and other measures of pay, see W. M. Conboy and D. Robinson, 'Wage Structures and Internal Labour Markets', in D. Robinson (ed.), *Local Labour Markets and Wage Structures* (London: Gower, 1970), pp. 215-18.

4. No examples of the components of pay of Linotype Operators and Piece Case Hands have been given because workers in these occupations are paid by results and not by time. The payment system which is known as the London Scale of Prices has a long history, dating back to the end of the eighteenth century. The scale is a complex set of regulations covering the type set for the newspaper. Basically it relates payments to the number of 'ems' or characters produced. It rewards workers if the setting is difficult. Share prices, for example, are amongst the most highly paid forms of setting. It also compensates them if they are denied earnings opportunities by the use of display advertisements, the payments being known as 'fat'. The Scale lays down standard charges that apply to all the offices but these charges are then subject to 'negotiated' interpretations by the managements and chapels. The Depotmen on the two evening newspapers (they are included within the category Publishing: Outdoor) are also paid commission depending on the number of copies sold.

5. Ideally, of course, a measure of pay should reflect the total package of benefits from employment. The EIU Report does contain some details about fringe benefits, but no comparisons can be made over time.

large differences in each of the years studied.[6] For example, Table 2.1, which gives details of the dispersion or scatter of earnings of 'All Occupations' (i.e. the weighted average for each office), shows that there was no year in which the range was less than 50%.[7] The coefficients of variation in column 3 are also large, indicating that the differences were not only at the extremes of the range.[8] It is also clear from Table 2.1 that the differences were not a temporary phenomenon. The dispersion was relatively stable in the first three years, the ranges and coefficients of variation showing little change. However, in 1970 both measures increased slightly.

TABLE 2.1
INTER-OFFICE EARNINGS DIFFERENTIALS
ALL OCCUPATIONS

	No. of Offices	Range (%)	Coefficient of Variation (%)	Weighted Average (£)
1961	10	52.8	14.8	28.13
1964	10	55.0	16.8	35.19
1967	10	55.8	16.0	38.93
1970	10	76.8	18.8	53.11

Table 2.2 underlines the size of the differences in earnings between offices by showing the distributions of the earnings ranges

6. The findings in Table 2.1 may be compared with those of MacKay *et al.* for the engineering industry in Birmingham and Glasgow. Using gross earnings, they found the spread of earnings in 'All Occupations' to be:

		June 1959	October 1966
Glasgow	Range	70.6	70.2
	Coefficient of Variation	13.8	12.1

		June 1963	June 1966
Birmingham	Range	75.2	47.7
	Coefficient of Variation	14.5	12.8

D. I. MacKay *et al.*, *Labour Markets under Different Employment Conditions* (London: Allen and Unwin, 1971), pp. 71 and 72.
7. The range is simply the difference between the lowest and highest paying offices expressed as a percentage of the lowest.
8. The coefficient of variation measures the relative dispersion of earnings of each office. It is the standard deviation divided by the mean and expressed as a percentage.

by occupation. Again, there are few examples of occupations for which the range was less than 50%; and at the other extreme there are some for which the range was more than 100%.

Unlike 'All Occupations', however, there was no common pattern from year to year in the case of the individual occupations. This becomes clear from Tables 2.3 to 2.6 which set out the details of the inter-office earnings differentials of the twenty-five occupations in each of the four years. For example, the dispersion increased each year in the case of Stereotypers; increased in 1970 in the case of most of the occupations in the composing and reading departments; and decreased in 1970 in the case of the occupations in the machine, publishing, and maintenance departments.

The findings of MacKay and his colleagues that the dispersion of earnings in the engineering industry tended to be larger in the case of skilled occupations does not seem to be true of Fleet Street.[9] It can be seen from Tables 2.3 to 2.6 that the dispersion was large in the case of some skilled occupations (defining 'skilled' here as the possession of an apprenticeship qualification). The Linotype Operators and Piece Case Hands, who are paid by results, had two of the largest scatters in each year. However, in the case of some skilled occupations there was very little dispersion; the Process Workers, for example, had one of the smallest scatters in each year. In Fleet Street the distinguishing characteristic appears to be the department. In other words, it seems that if the dispersion is large in one occupation in a department, it tends to be equally large in other occupations in that department. Again, Tables 2.3 to 2.6 illustrate the point in the case of the occupations in the machine and maintenance departments.

Ranking of Offices

In view of the large differences in earnings between the offices, it might be thought that there would be little change in their ranking. For example, MacKay and his colleagues found in the engineering industry that although the rank orders of earnings were less stable using gross as distinct from standard earnings, major changes were usually reversed over a longer period.[10] But Table 2.7, which gives

9. MacKay *et al., op. cit.*, p. 74.
10. *ibid.*, p. 83.

TABLE 2.2

DISTRIBUTION OF EARNINGS RANGES BY OCCUPATION

	% Less than 25%	% 25.0 29.9	% 30.0 34.9	% 35.0 39.9	% 40.0 44.9	% 45.0 49.9	% 50.0 54.9	% 55.0 59.9	% 60.0 64.9	% 65.0 69.9	% 70.0 74.9	% 75.0 79.9	% 80.0 84.9	% 85.0 89.9	% 90.0 94.9	% 95.0 99.9	% 100 or more	Number of Occupations
1961	2		2		1	2	2	3	1	3	7		3				1	25
1964			1	1	1	2	2		3	2	2	2	1		1	1	4	25
1967		1			2	3	1	3	2		1	1		2	3	1	5	25
1970	1		1	2	1	1	1	1	3	4	1	1	4		2		3	25

TABLE 2.3

INTER-OFFICE EARNINGS DIFFERENTIALS: OCTOBER 1961

Occupation	No. of Offices	Range: Lowest to Highest %	Coefficient Variation	Weighted Average (£)
Wireroom Operators	5	59.6	17.8	26.35
Telephoto Operators	5	30.6	11.4	29.99
Photoprinters	8	47.8	16.3	20.37
Permanent Time Hands	10	30.5	9.7	27.50
Linotype Operators	10	80.5	19.1	37.04
Piece Case Hands	10	125.2	21.7	41.46
Proof Pullers	10	51.7	12.6	20.23
Linotype Assistants	10	67.4	14.8	21.10
Readers	10	52.0	14.1	27.07
Revisers	10	72.7	16.2	20.59
Copyreaders	10	71.3	17.7	18.55
Process Workers	8	41.0	11.4	32.56
Stereotypers	10	69.5	17.0	39.02
Machine Managers	10	74.4	21.1	34.05
Brake Hands	10	71.8	19.9	31.12
Magazine Hands	10	82.4	20.2	29.24
Oilers	10	73.8	19.8	29.14
General Assistants	10	74.5	18.7	29.04
Publishing: Indoor	10	55.3	15.8	25.48
Publishing: Outdoor	10	73.8	20.1	24.86
Engineers	8	82.0	22.9	29.29
Engineers' Assistants	6	68.5	16.9	18.99
Electricians	8	61.7	14.2	27.14
Electricians' Assistants	6	57.4	15.9	21.04
Messengers/Doormen Cleaners/Firemen	8	45.1	14.1	17.33
All Occupations	10	52.8	14.8	28.13

TABLE 2.4

INTER-OFFICE EARNINGS DIFFERENTIALS: OCTOBER 1964

Occupation	No. of Offices	Range: Lowest to Highest %	Coefficient Variation	Weighted Average (£)
Wireroom Operators	5	33.9	13.2	38.72
Telephoto Operators	5	19.4	7.2	34.14
Photoprinters	8	61.2	15.1	26.11
Permanent Time Hands	10	49.2	13.0	33.97
Linotype Operators	10	111.2	23.7	45.07
Piece Case Hands	10	118.5	23.2	46.73
Proof Pullers	10	43.6	12.1	26.75
Linotype Assistants	10	51.8	13.6	27.38
Readers	10	51.5	13.4	35.31
Revisers	10	75.6	16.2	28.70
Copyreaders	10	47.6	11.3	25.02
Process Workers	8	24.5	7.2	38.98
Stereotypers	10	94.4	22.5	46.34
Machine Managers	10	67.2	19.2	42.68
Brake Hands	10	72.9	21.9	37.55
Magazine Hands	10	73.3	20.6	35.70
Oilers	10	60.7	19.0	36.02
General Assistants	10	67.1	19.5	35.96
Publishing: Indoor	10	79.1	18.7	32.95
Publishing: Outdoor	10	81.6	22.3	33.59
Engineers	8	105.9	26.7	36.62
Engineers' Assistants	6	61.1	18.3	24.89
Electricians	8	96.3	24.8	34.58
Electricians' Assistants	7	105.3	30.1	25.00
Messengers/Doormen Cleaners/Firemen	8	37.6	13.2	21.92
All Occupations	10	55.0	16.8	35.19

TABLE 2.5

INTER-OFFICE EARNINGS DIFFERENTIALS: OCTOBER 1967

Occupation	No. of Offices	Range: Lowest to Highest %	Coefficient Variation	Weighted Average (£)
Wireroom Operators	5	46.0	14.4	40.84
Telephoto Operators	5	42.5	12.5	39.08
Photoprinters	8	43.8	13.8	30.61
Permanent Time Hands	10	55.8	11.7	40.41
Linotype Operators	10	95.7	20.3	51.82
Piece Case Hands	10	78.3	16.1	53.23
Proof Pullers	10	48.8	11.8	31.76
Linotype Assistants	9	61.6	12.1	33.20
Readers	10	52.9	12.1	38.55
Revisers	10	90.5	18.8	33.09
Copyreaders	10	61.6	14.8	29.19
Process Workers	8	28.3	8.3	40.60
Stereotypers	10	117.4	25.5	48.39
Machine Managers	10	88.1	24.5	44.04
Brake Hands	10	112.5	23.2	38.13
Magazine Hands	10	110.6	23.0	37.22
Oilers	10	119.9	24.1	36.88
General Assistants	10	87.6	19.9	36.53
Publishing: Indoor	10	59.1	15.0	36.03
Publishing: Outdoor	9	71.7	19.7	34.85
Engineers	8	104.8	24.8	50.52
Engineers' Assistants	6	58.6	18.7	29.16
Electricians	8	94.6	23.6	42.80
Electricians' Assistants	6	94.2	32.0	32.07
Messengers/Doormen Cleaners/Firemen	8	45.7	12.4	25.01
All Occupations	10	55.8	16.0	38.93

TABLE 2.6

INTER-OFFICE EARNINGS DIFFERENTIALS: OCTOBER 1970

Occupation	No. of Offices	Range: Lowest to Highest %	Coefficient Variation	Weighted Average (£)
Wireroom Operators	4 *	37.2	15.7	52.04
Telephoto Operators	4 *	66.4	22.2	49.83
Photoprinters	5 *	45.4	15.9	46.61
Permanent Time Hands	10	84.3	16.6	57.05
Linotype Operators	10	122.5	22.0	71.16
Piece Case Hands	10	86.6	16.0	71.18
Proof Pullers	10	81.6	17.3	43.04
Linotype Assistants	10	66.6	13.6	42.47
Readers	10	93.8	18.6	56.35
Revisers	10	107.8	20.7	48.64
Copyreaders	10	70.3	14.4	42.51
Process Workers	8	56.9	13.1	51.99
Stereotypers	10	121.5	26.5	60.90
Machine Managers	10	68.4	20.6	60.30
Brake Hands	10	91.5	20.4	50.63
Magazine Hands	10	80.5	19.0	47.85
Oilers	10	83.8	18.6	48.34
General Assistants	10	76.0	18.9	51.00
Publishing: Indoor	10	50.6	14.8	45.93
Publishing: Outdoor	9	69.5	16.9	44.05
Engineers	8	64.6	17.0	64.69
Engineers' Assistants	5 *	42.8	15.8	48.21
Electricians	8	38.6	15.4	63.97
Electricians' Assistants	6	60.4	16.4	40.54
Messengers/Doormen Cleaners/Firemen	4 *	21.9	8.9	33.97
All Occupations	10	76.8	18.8	53.11

* Details for these occupations are incomplete

23

TABLE 2.7

RANKING OF OFFICES BY AVERAGE WEEKLY
EARNINGS: SELECTED OCCUPATIONS

Office Number	All Occupations				Permanent Time Hands				Linotype Operators				Readers				Copy Readers			
	1961	1964	1967	1970	1961	1964	1967	1970	1961	1964	1967	1970	1961	1964	1967	1970	1961	1964	1967	1970
A	2	3	1	1	1	1	1	1	1	1	1	1	6	5	1	1	5	5	1	1
B	3	2	2	2	2	3	2	3	6	7	8	8	5	7	7	7	6	8	8	5
C	1	1	3	3	3	2	7	9	5	4	6	5	1	2	3	9	2	3	2	9
D	4	5	5	5	4	5	8	4	3	5	3	5	2	1	2	6	1	1	4	7
E	7	10	8	8	5	9	3	2	4	6	5	4	9	9	6	3	9	9	7	3
F	9	6	10	10	6	7	9	8	8	8	9	9	3	3	9	8	3	2	6	8
G	10	9	9	9	7	8	4	6	7	3	2	3	7	8	5	4	7	7	3	4
H	5	4	6	6	8	4	5	5	2	2	4	7	8	4	8	2	8	6	9	2
I	8	8	7	7	9	10	10	10	10	10	10	10	10	10	10	10	10	10	10	10
J	6	7	4	4	10	6	6	7	9	9	7	2	4	6	4	5	4	4	5	6
Rank Correlation	.8454	.9030	.8424		.6727	.5152	.5758		.8424	.7576	.4002		.9347	.5030	.3091		.9394	.6364	.2848	

TABLE 2.7 (Continued)

Office Number	Stereotypers				Machine Managers				General Assistants				Publishing: Indoor			
	1961	1964	1967	1970	1961	1964	1967	1970	1961	1964	1967	1970	1961	1963	1967	1970
A	1	1	1	1	3	3	3	3	7	4	4	2	9	7	3	2
B	2	2	2	2	2	1	2	1	2	2	2	1	2	1	1	1
C	3	3	3	5	1	2	4	4	1	1	3	3	1	2	2	4
D	5	4	5	6	6	6	5	7	5	6	7	7	7	3	7	6
E	10	10	9	4	5	8	6	8	4	7	6	6	10	10	10	7
F	4	6	7	8	7	4	10	6	10	8	10	10	5	4	5	8
G	7	7	8	9	10	10	9	10	8	10	9	9	4	6	8	10
H	9	8	10	10	8	7	7	3	9	3	8	5	6	8	9	5
I	4	5	6	7	9	9	8	9	6	9	5	8	3	5	6	9
J	6	9	4	3	4	5	1	5	3	5	1	4	8	9	4	3
Rank Correlation	.9102	.8851	.5085		.8667	.8061	.7054		.2708	.6278	.4308		.7818	.4667	.0667–	

details of the ranking offices by average weekly earnings, shows that it was not unusual for the offices in Fleet Street to change their position; and the highest and lowest paying offices were not always the same ones. The rank correlation coefficients, which are a measure of the stability between two rank orders, are positive and significant at the 5% level in the case of 'All Occupations'.[11] However, in a number of the individual occupations many of the coefficients are not significant at this level. Indeed, the coefficient in the case of Publishing: Indoor is not even positive in 1970. As has already been pointed out, this is all the more surprising in view of the large differences in earnings in the base period.[12]

Table 2.7 also suggests that the offices were similarly placed in the different rank orders of occupational earnings. So it would appear that if changes took place in one rank order they took place in others as well. The next chapter, which describes the internal pay structures of the different offices, will have more to say about this.

To summarize the findings so far, there were large differences in earnings between the offices in each year studied, and yet it was not unusual for offices to change position in the rank orders of earnings.

11. Correlation coefficients provide a useful test of the strength of the relationship between two or more variables which are thought for other reasons to be associated with one another. They are expressed within the range —1 to +1. If the coefficients are positive, high values of one variable are associated with high values of the other. If, on the other hand, the coefficients are negative, high values of one are associated with low values of the other. The closer the coefficients are to —1 or +1, the stronger they are. The coefficients are usually said to be 'significant' when there is only a one in twenty possibility that the result has occurred by chance, i.e. at the 5% level. The rank correlation coefficient is therefore a measure of the agreement between two rank orders.
12. MacKay, for example, writes: 'Hence the interplant wage structure retains a high degree of stability over fairly long periods of time not because changes in earnings are the same from unit to unit but because the difference in earnings' levels are so sustained in the base period that large differences in earnings' changes can be accommodated with relatively little effect on the wage hierarchy.' D. I. MacKay, 'Wages and Labour Turnover', in D. Robinson (ed.), *op. cit.*

Chapter 3

The Internal Pay Structures

Occupational Differentials

Following the description of the large differences in earnings between offices in the last chapter, Fleet Street might be expected to vindicate the statement that 'the outstanding characteristic of the earnings relativities in any plant is its uniqueness; there are as many intra-plant earnings structures as plants'.[1] Tables 3.1 to 3.4, which show the distribution of occupational earnings differentials by office (ranked in order of industry basic rates), give some support to this statement. In some occupations, for example, there were no offices within a range of 5% of each other. However, Tables 3.1 to 3.4 also suggest that there were a number of similarities between the offices. With the exception of the occupations in the machine department, which enjoyed a slightly higher position in some offices, the rank orders of occupational earnings generally followed the rank order of industry basic rates.[2] There were also several occupations in which the differentials for four of the offices fell within a range of 5% of each other, and there were others in which a majority of the offices fell within a range of 10%. Finally, with the exception of the Engineers and Electricians, who improved their relative position, there was a narrowing of differentials between 1961 and 1970.[3]

The narrowing in differentials shows up much more clearly in

1. D. I. MacKay *et al., Labour Markets Under Different Employment Conditions* (London: Allen and Unwin, 1971), p. 118. This is the conclusion to which most empirical studies of pay structure have come. See also H. A. Turner *et al., Labour Relations in the Motor Industry* (London: Allen and Unwin, 1967).
2. MacKay *et al.* also found that occupational earnings differentials corresponded with a skill hierarchy when time workers and piece workers were treated as separate groups, *op. cit.*, p. 114.
3. MacKay *et al.* also found that there was a tendency for lower-paid workers to improve their relative position. *ibid.*, p. 126.

TABLE 3.1

DISTRIBUTION OF OCCUPATIONAL DIFFERENTIALS BY OFFICE
(Average Weekly Earnings as a percentage of the Earnings of 'All Occupations'):
SELECTED OCCUPATIONS, 1961

	50.0–54.9%	55.0–59.9%	60.0–64.9%	65.0–69.9%	70.0–74.9%	75.0–79.9%	80.0–84.9%	85.0–89.9%	90.0–94.9%	95.0–99.9%	100.0–4.9%	5.0–9.9%	10.0–14.9%	15.0–19.9%	20.0–24.9%	25.0–29.9%	30.0–34.9%	35.0–39.9%	40.0–44.9%	45.0–49.9%	50.0–54.9%	55.0–59.9%	60%	Number of Offices
Copyreaders	2	2	2	1			1		2															10
General Assistants							2		1	1	2	2	2											10
Publishing: Indoor			1				3	1	4	1														10
Machine Managers							1						3	1	1		4							10
Engineers									1		1		2	2		1		1						8
Electricians					1					1	3	1	1	1										8
Process Workers							1		1	1	1		1	1			1	1						8
Readers						2	1	3		2		1				1								10
Permanent Time Hands							1		3	2	1	3												10
Stereotypers														1	2			2	2		1	2		10
Linotype Operators										1		1	1	1				2	1	1	1		1	10

TABLE 3.2

DISTRIBUTION OF OCCUPATIONAL DIFFERENTIALS BY OFFICE
(Average Weekly Earnings as a percentage of the Earnings of 'All Occupations'):
SELECTED OCCUPATIONS, 1964

	50.0%–54.9%	55.0%–59.9%	60.0%–64.9%	65.0%–69.9%	70.0%–74.9%	75.0%–79.9%	80.0%–84.9%	85.0%–89.9%	90.0%–94.9%	95.0%–99.9%	100.0%–4.9%	5.0%–9.9%	10.0%–14.9%	15.0%–19.9%	20.0%–24.9%	25.0%–29.9%	30.0%–34.9%	35.0%–39.9%	40.0%–44.9%	45.0%–49.9%	50.0%–54.9%	55.0%–59.9%	60%	Number of Offices
Copyreaders	1	1	2	1		1	2	2																10
General Assistants			1						3	2	1	3												10
Publishing: Indoor				1		1		3	2	2	1													10
Machine Managers												1		4	2	1	1	1						10
Process Workers									2	1	2		2				1							8
Readers								1	2		2	1	1		2	1								10
Permanent Time Hands							1	2	1	3	3													10
Engineers									2		1		1	1		3								8
Electricians					1		1		3			1	1	1										8
Stereotypers															2	2		4		1			1	10
Linotype Operators									1		2			2		1		1					3	10

TABLE 3.3

DISTRIBUTION OF OCCUPATIONAL DIFFERENTIALS BY OFFICE

(Average Weekly Earnings as a percentage of the Earnings of 'All Occupations'):
SELECTED OCCUPATIONS, 1967

	50.0% 54.9%	55.0% 59.9%	60.0% 64.9%	65.0% 69.9%	70.0% 74.9%	75.0% 79.9%	80.0% 84.9%	85.0% 89.9%	90.0% 94.9%	95.0% 99.9%	100.0% 4.9%	5.0% 9.9%	10.0% 14.9%	15.0% 19.9%	20.0% 24.9%	25.0% 29.9%	30.0% 34.9%	35.0% 39.9%	40.0% 44.9%	45.0% 49.9%	50.0% 54.9%	55.0% 59.9%	60%	Number of Offices
Copyreaders	1			1	4	1	2		1															10
General Assistants					1	1		2	1	1	3			1										10
Publishing: Indoor						1		4	1	2	1	1												10
Machine Managers											1	4	2	1		1						1		10
Process Workers								1	1		1	4					1							8
Readers						1	1	1	1	1	1	2	2											10
Permanent Time-Hands									3	2	1	1	1	1	1									10
Stereotypers											1	1		1	3	2	1				1			10
Engineers													2			1		1	1	1	2			8
Electricians						1				1		3		1		1		1						8
Linotype Operators										1		1	2			1	1		1	2			1	10

TABLE 3.4

DISTRIBUTION OF OCCUPATIONAL DIFFERENTIALS BY OFFICE
(Average Weekly Earnings as a percentage of the Earnings of 'All Occupations'):
SELECTED OCCUPATIONS, 1970

	50.0%/54.9%	55.0%/59.9%	60.0%/64.9%	65.0%/69.9%	70.0%/74.9%	75.0%/79.9%	80.0%/84.9%	85.0%/89.9%	90.0%/94.9%	95.0%/99.9%	100.0%/4.9%	5.0%/9.9%	10.0%/14.9%	15.0%/19.9%	20.0%/24.9%	25.0%/29.9%	30.0%/34.9%	35.0%/39.9%	40.0%/44.9%	45.0%/49.9%	50.0%/54.9%	55.0%/59.9%	60%	Number of Offices
Copyreaders				3	1	1	1	2	1		1													10
General Assistants							2	1	2	4	1													10
Publishing: Indoor					1		1	4	3	1														10
Machine Managers											3	1		2	1	1		1	1					10
Process Workers	1						1	1			1	1	1	1	1									8
Readers								2		2	1	2	2			1								10
Permanent Time Hands									1	3	2	2			2									10
Stereotypers								1				1	1	3	2		2							10
Engineers														1	2	1	2	1	1					8
Electricians														1	2	1	1	1	1	1				8
Linotype Operators											1	1	3		1		3		1					10

Table 3.5 which gives measures of the dispersion of earnings between occupations and within offices. It can be seen from column 1 that there was a distinct narrowing in the dispersion of earnings between the average of the different occupations. Column 2 suggests a similar tendency in the case of differentials between occupations in the same office: that is, for the internal pay structures to be compressed.

TABLE 3.5

DISPERSION OF EARNINGS: BY OCCUPATION AND OFFICE

	Dispersion of Earnings between the average for each Occupation Coefficient of Variation	Dispersion of Earnings between Occupations within each Office Average Coefficient of Variation
1961	24.2	27.9
1964	20.8	23.9
1967	19.0	23.2
1970	17.7	21.2

The similarities between the offices are much more marked at the level of the department. Table 3.6, which shows the distribution of occupational differentials in the machine department by office, confirms that it was extremely rare for the rank order of industry

TABLE 3.6

DISTRIBUTION OF OCCUPATIONAL DIFFERENTIALS BY OFFICE:
MACHINE DEPARTMENT (Average Weekly Earnings of Brake Hands and General Assistants as a percentage of those of Machine Managers)

		60.0 % 64.9	65.0 % 69.9	70.0 % 74.9	75.0 % 79.9	80.0 % 84.9	85.0 % 89.9	90.0 % 94.9	95.0 % 99.9	100.0 + %	Number of Offices
	1961		1		*	1	4	3		1	10
Brake	1964			2		1*	5		1	1	10
Hands	1967				2	*	5	2		1	10
	1970	1	1			*	6			2	10
	1961	1		1	2*	3	1	1	1		10
General	1964	1		1	3*	2	3				10
Assistants	1967			3	1*	2	1	2		1	10
	1970	1	1		2*	4		2			10

*Denotes differential in industry basic rate

32

basic rates to be reversed. There were only two offices in which Brake Hands earned more than Machine Managers and only one office, in 1970, in which General Assistants earned more. There are also similarities between the offices in the size of the differentials. The Brake Hands' differential, for example, fell within a range of 10% in seven of the offices in both 1961 and 1967.

TABLE 3.7
DISTRIBUTION OF OCCUPATIONAL DIFFERENTIALS BY OFFICE:
READING DEPARTMENT (Average Weekly Earnings of Revisers and
Copyreaders as a percentage of those of Readers)

		60.0 % 64.9	65.0 % 69.9	70.0 % 74.9	75.0 % 79.9	80.0 % 84.9	85.0 % 89.9	90.0 % 94.9	95.0 % 99.9	100.0+ %	Number of Offices
Revisers	1961	1		3*	2	3	1				10
	1964			3*	3	2	1	1			10
	1967			1*	5		2	2			10
	1970				*	4	5		1		10
Copy- readers	1961		5*	4		1					10
	1964		3*	5	2						10
	1967		1	3*	4	2					10
	1970		1	4*	5						10

*Denotes differential in industry basic rate

Table 3.7, which shows the distribution of occupational differentials in the reading department, reveals a similar pattern. There were no offices in which the rank order of industry basic rates was reversed. Also, the differentials of both Revisers and Copyreaders fell within a range of 10% in nine offices in 1970. However, there was one difference between the situations in the machine and reading departments. Differentials did not narrow noticeably in the machine department, but there was a distinct narrowing in the reading department in most offices.[4] In 1961 Revisers earned less than 80% of Readers' earnings in six offices; but in 1970 Revisers' earnings did not fall below that level in any office.

4. Significantly, there were very few offices in which the differential narrowed in absolute terms.

TABLE 3.8

DISTRIBUTION OF PERCENTAGE CHANGES IN EARNINGS BY OFFICE: SELECTED OCCUPATIONS, 1961-70

	Less than 25.0%	25.0%–29.9	30.0%–34.9	35.0%–39.9	40.0%–44.9	45.0%–49.9	50.0%–54.9	55.0%–59.9	60.0%–64.9	65.0%–69.9	70.0%–74.9	75.0%–79.9	80.0%–84.9	85.0%–89.9	90.0%–94.9	95.0%–99.9	100.0%–104.9	105.0%–109.9	110.0%–114.9	115.0%–119.9
Process Workers			1	*				2	1	1	3									
Permanent Time Hands				*						2					1		1		1	
Readers					1					1		1		1				1		
Machine Managers			1	*			1			1		2	1		1		1			
Stereotypers			2		1*		1		2						1	1	1			
Publishing: Indoor					*		1	1	1				1	2		1			1	
General Assistants						1*			1	2		3			1					
Copyreaders						*				1						1		1		
Electricians							*											1		3
Engineers							*						2					1		
Linotype Operators			1				1		1				2		1	2			1	

*Denotes change in industry basic rate.

TABLE 3.6 (Continued)

	120.0 %124.9	125.0 %129.9	130.0 %134.9	135.0 %139.9	140.0 %144.9	145.0 %149.9	150.0 %154.9	155.0 %159.9	160.0 %164.9	165.0 %169.9	170.0 %174.9	175.0 %179.9	180.0 %184.9	185.0 %189.9	190.0 %194.9	195.0 %199.9	200.0+ %
Process Workers																	
Permanent Time Hands	1	1		2													1
Readers			1					1	1								
Machine Managers								1									
Stereotypers																	
Publishing: Indoor			1							1							
General Assistants	1			1			2										
Copyreaders	1								2						1	2	
Electricians	1						1				1						
Engineers	1	3															
Linotype Operators							1										

* Denotes change in industry basic rate.

FIGURE 3.1
CHANGES IN EARNINGS: ALL OCCUPATIONS

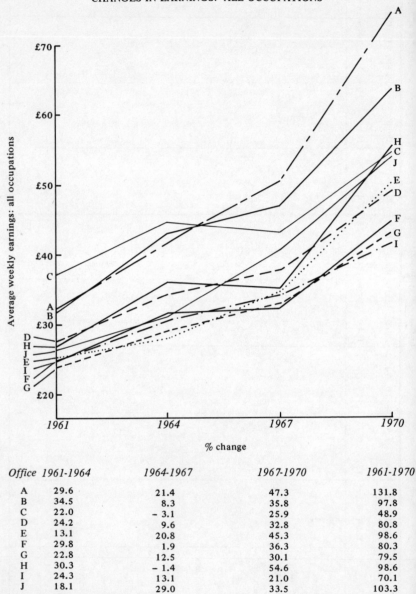

% change

Office	1961-1964	1964-1967	1967-1970	1961-1970
A	29.6	21.4	47.3	131.8
B	34.5	8.3	35.8	97.8
C	22.0	- 3.1	25.9	48.9
D	24.2	9.6	32.8	80.8
E	13.1	20.8	45.3	98.6
F	29.8	1.9	36.3	80.3
G	22.8	12.5	30.1	79.5
H	30.3	- 1.4	54.6	98.6
I	24.3	13.1	21.0	70.1
J	18.1	29.0	33.5	103.3

36

Changes in Earnings

Taken with those of the previous chapter, these findings appear to present something of a paradox. There were large differences in earnings between the offices, and yet there were also a number of similarities between the rank orders of occupational earnings and in the size of the occupational earnings differentials which narrowed in most offices. The paradox is further illustrated in Figure 3.1 and Table 3.8. Figure 3.1, which gives details of the changes in the earnings of 'All Occupations', shows that there was a common trend in several offices. Except for office J, earnings rose much less in the period 1964 to 1967 than in the other two periods; in two offices they actually fell. It also shows that changes in earnings in some offices kept in step over the period. A and C, for example, were among those with the highest and lowest increases respectively in all three periods. But the most remarkable feature revealed by Figure 3.1 is the erratic behaviour of other offices. J, for example, had the lowest increase in earnings in the period 1961 to 1964 and the highest in the period 1964 to 1967; H had the second highest increase in the period 1961 to 1964, the second highest *decrease* in the period 1964 to 1967, and the highest increase in the period 1967 to 1970.

By contrast, Table 3.8, which shows the distribution of percentage changes in the earnings of selected occupations, reveals notable similarities between the offices at the level of the department and occupation. There were no offices in which Process Workers received increases above 75% or Stereotypers received increases over 100%; there were only two offices in which Machine Managers and Publishing: Indoor received more than 100%. At the other end of the range, there were no offices in which Electricians received increases *less* than 100%, and only two in which Engineers received *less* than 100%, and there were only four in which Readers and Copyreaders received *less* than 100%.

In short, the explanation of the paradox must be that the occupation exerted as much influence over a man's earnings as the office in which he worked. This proposition was tested by the analysis of variance which is discussed in more detail in Chapter 8 and it is sufficient to note here that it was confirmed.

Postscript

It follows that the internal pay structures in Fleet Street cannot be treated as entirely separate entities. It is more realistic to think in terms of a number of pay structures in each office — following Dunlop, these might be called 'job clusters' — which lie within two 'wage contours', one determined by the office and the other by the occupation.[5] How applicable this approach is to other situations must be a matter for further research. It has the disadvantage that the boundaries of an internal pay structure cannot be defined *a priori*. But, then, the traditional approach too is suspect because it depends on the researcher's definition which might not be the same as that of the parties involved. To cite an example: the finding of most empirical studies that the earnings relativities in any plant are unique might result simply from representing the earnings of different occupations as a percentage of the earnings of labourers, whereas workers in these occupations might not regard the relationship with labourers as significant.[6] Chapter 8 will have more to say about this.

Despite the large differences in earnings between offices, therefore, there were similarities between the rank orders of earnings and in the size of the occupational earnings differentials. It is noticeable too that changes in earnings followed common trends in several offices and occupational earnings differentials narrowed in most.

5. See J. T. Dunlop, 'The Task of Contemporary Wage Theory', in F. E. Pierson and G. W. Taylor (eds.), *New Concepts in Wage Determination* (New York: McGraw Hill, 1957).
6. MacKay *et al.* and Conboy and Robinson measure occupational earnings differentials by representing the earnings of different occupations as a percentage of the earnings of labourers.

Chapter 4

The Components of Pay

Components of Pay Negotiated by NPA and Trade Unions

There is hardly any need to justify an examination of the significance of the components of pay negotiated by the NPA and the trade unions. The industry basic rates in Table 4.1 which are negotiated by the NPA and those unions listed in the Introduction, are applied in each office and form the foundation for other components. There are more than thirty occupations mentioned in these agreements, most with different rates.[1] There are also different rates depending on the category of newspaper and the shift. In total there are some seventy different rates.

The cost of living bonus to which reference is made in Table 4.1 was paid to all the occupations included in the study with the exception of the Engineers, Electricians, and Electricians' Assistants (and Process Workers, 1961 to 1964). The bonus, which was related to the index of retail prices by a sliding scale, was adjusted quarterly; an increase of one point was valued at 10p. Sums amounting to 30p were absorbed into the industry basic rates at periodic intervals depending on the level of the index. The sliding scale was discontinued in 1968 and the outstanding bonus later absorbed into the industry basic rates.

Like the industry basic rates, the extras shown in Table 4.2 are negotiated by the NPA and the different unions. However, there is one important difference: these extras are only paid when the particular task is performed or the circumstances are those for which the payment has been agreed. Two broad categories may be

---

1. This coverage is very different from that, say, in the engineering industry where negotiations between the employers' association and trade unions settle only a minimum frame-work of industry basic rates. See A. Marsh, *Industrial Relations in Engineering* (Oxford: Pergamon Press, 1965), p. 11.

TABLE 4.2

INDUSTRY EXTRAS (NEGOTIATED BY NPA AND TRADE UNIONS)

Press Telegraphists

Weekly extra of 6% minimum time rate for men required to undertake work for more than one NPA paper and for mixed work (which may be defined as work not connected with the contents of the paper).

Photographic Printers

Weekly extra of 6% minimum time rate for men working on the Sunday paper in a dual office.

Permanent Time Hands

Weekly extra of 6% minimum time rate for men working on the Sunday paper in a dual office. Weekly extras paid for special responsibilities as follows:

Page make-up	8.4% minimum time rate
Random desk	13.0% minimum time rate
Copy desk/marking-up	15.0% minimum time rate

Readers/Revisers/Copyreaders

Weekly extra of 6% minimum time rate for men working on the Sunday paper in a dual office.

A 'comprehensive extra duties' payment of 7% of the minimum time rate to all readers.

Men required to work for more than one NPA paper during the week receive extras as follows:

Men employed primarily on one paper who are required to assist on the production of one other to receive an extra 13.77% of the minimum time rate. The same extra is paid to men primarily employed on two daily papers with fully established joint staff.

Men primarily employed on one morning paper who are required to assist in the production of two other papers or who are employed on one daily paper with recognized interchangeability of work and rotas with another daily paper and who are also required to assist in the production of a Sunday paper receive an extra 26.88% of the minimum time rate.

Stereotypers

Men required to work on a Sunday paper during the week receive 6% of the minimum time rate.

Men involved in the simultaneous production of two or more papers receive 8.833% of the minimum time rate.

Men involved in the production of pre-printed photogravure colour receive 3.05% of the minimum time rate.

Machine Managers

Men involved in work on seals, fudges, receive an extra as follows:

On a morning paper	4% of the time rate
On an evening paper	7% of the time rate
On a Sunday paper	2% of the time rate

in advertisements in colour:

Evening and morning papers	3s. per advertisement
Sunday papers	4s.6d. per advertisement

Men involved in the production of pre-printed photogravure colour receive 5.25% of the minimum time rate when half or more of the presses are used, and half payment when less.

41

TABLE 4.2 (Continued)

Machine Assistants

Men involved in the production of pre-printed photogravure colour receive 3.9% of the General Assistants' time rate when half or more of the presses are used, and half when less.

Engineers/Electricians

Men involved in registered pre-printed photogravure colour receive an extra of 1.9% of the minimum time rate.

distinguished. Some are applied generally and follow the negotiation of the industry basic rates. Bank holiday extras are an example. Others, which are peculiar to one occupation or group of occupations, are the result of negotiations between the NPA and an individual union which has submitted a so-called 'domestic'[2] claim on behalf of its members or some section of them. The 'Sunday paper extra' in the example in Table 4.3 falls into this category. In both cases the extras are calculated from the industry basic rates but do not usually count for overtime.

The previous chapter has already observed that the rank order of industry basic rates and the size of the occupational differentials in these rates had some effect on the rank orders of earnings and the size of the occupational earnings differentials. But there is little evidence in Tables 4.1 and 4.2 to suggest that the components of pay negotiated by the NPA and the trade unions were significant for the other findings in Chapters 2 and 3. For example, the differences in the industry basic rates of the same occupation which are shown in Table 4.1 cannot explain the differences in earnings between offices described in Chapter 2. Of the ten offices included in the study, eight printed daily newspapers and so paid the same or similar industry basic rates. Furthermore, in the case of most occupations both the lowest and highest paying offices printed daily newspapers. Differences in the payment of extras might have been significant but this is a possibility which will be taken up later.

It is also clear from Table 4.1 that the timing and amount of increases in the industry basic rates (and extras) cannot wholly explain the findings in Chapter 3. First, the slight reduction in the occupational differentials in these rates is not sufficient to explain the extent of the decrease in occupational earnings differentials. Second, the increases in these rates, some of which have already

2. This usage of the term is peculiar to the printing and newspaper industry.

been shown in Table 3.8, cannot explain the differences in the changes in earnings by office and by occupation; in fact, there were reductions in earnings in a number of cases. Finally, since most of the occupations received it, the cost of living bonus cannot be regarded as significant either. (However, the fact that Engineers and Electricians did not receive the bonus enabled them to argue for interim increases in the industry basic rates.) Indeed, it is the absence of major changes in the structure of the industry basic rates and the other components of pay negotiated by the NPA and the trade unions which must be explained.

Components of Pay Negotiated by Managements and Chapels

The size of the earnings gap in the example in Table 4.3, which is

TABLE 4.3

THE COMPONENTS OF PAY: PHOTOPRINTERS, 1969

Components Negotiated by NPA and Trade Unions

	£	%
Basic	20.55	42.5
Cost of living bonus	1.10	2.3
Sunday paper extra	1.23	2.6
Saturday differential	.93	1.9
Bank holiday extra	.16	0.3

Components Negotiated by the Managements and Chapels

	£	%
Existing extraneous	3.15	6.5
New extraneous	1.53	3.2
Telephones	.58	1.2
Overtime in new rotas	1.42	2.9
Equated holiday/sick cover	3.48	7.2
Equated mobile overtime and office cover	4.65	9.6
Share of overtime no longer required on new rota	.78	1.6
Microfilming/Reader service	.80	1.7
Colour extra (12½% basic)	2.56	5.3
Missing man	1.43	3.0
Rota payment	1.02	2.1
Miscellaneous overtime	.66	1.4
Productivity payment	1.16	2.4
44/48p.p. Sunday paper	1.11	2.3
TOTAL	48.30	

43

typical of the make-up of pay of the occupations in the production and maintenance departments, underlines the significance of the components of pay negotiated by the managements and the chapels. But it is by no means exceptional. In fact, in one case earnings in 1970 were almost four times the industry basic rate.

The difficulties in treating overtime payments have already been touched on in the introduction to this part of the study. Three categories of overtime payment can be distinguished. First, there are the payments for irregular overtime which is actually worked to meet exceptional circumstances in production or distribution. There are no examples of this category in Table 4.3. Second, there are payments for regular, sometimes known as 'covenanted', overtime which is worked in part or whole each week. One example is the overtime which is required for an 'early start' in the machine department. Third, there are the payments which are made without the overtime being worked; these are straightforward bonuses and may be likened to the other 'house extras' described below. In one office, for example, the number of hours 'paid' to day machine assistants is related to the number of newsprint reels they bring into the office. They may be 'paid' for as many as seventy or eighty hours a week, but it is doubtful if they work the basic hours in the industry agreement because of the practice of 'job and finish'.

The 'productivity payment' referred to in Table 4.3 also deserves some comment. Payments such as this were a key feature of the comprehensive or productivity agreements which were negotiated by the managements and the chapels in this period. Better known as staff reduction payments, they represent the individual's share of the savings from a reduction in the number of jobs in a department. Later chapters will have more to say about the significance of comprehensive agreements,[3] but it is important to mention here one important consequence of the negotiation of this type of agreement. In most cases the components of pay were consolidated into a single 'comprehensive' or 'equated' weekly rate which is calculated over the income-tax year or half-year. But the components do not lose their former identity; they are listed much as in the example in Table 4.3 and may be adjusted in the light of increases in the industry basic rates.

3. See Chapters 8 and 10 for further details. See also Appendix I.

Earnings Drift

One method of establishing the *relative* significance of the components of pay negotiated by the managements and chapels is to investigate the extent of earnings drift, i.e. the change in the size of the earnings gap through time.[4] But there are a number of measures of drift. The simplest, referred to by the OME as the 'conventional' measure, is the percentage increase in earnings less the percentage increase in industry basic rates.[5] A second measure — and the one favoured by the NBPI — is the change through time in the size of the gap between earnings and industry basic rates.[6] Tables 4.4 to 4.6 use these measures to show the average annual drift for selected occupations over the periods 1961 to 1964, 1964 to 1967, and 1967 to 1970 respectively. In brackets is shown the proportion of increases in earnings which result from increases in the components of pay negotiated by the managements and chapels.

Like the 'conventional' measure, the 'NBPI' measure confirms the overriding significance of changes in the components of pay negotiated by the managements and chapels. However, in Fleet

4. The OME defines drift as follows: 'Wage drift is the term used to describe changes in the gap between earnings and rates through time. It may be expressed as the relationship between changes in the gap and wage rates or, alternatively, the difference between the rate of growth of earnings and wage rates. A distinction is also drawn in the literature between earnings drift which includes the effects of overtime payments, and wage drift, which excludes them . . .' OME, *Wage Drift: Review of Literature and Research* (London: HMSO, 1973), p. 3.
5. *op. cit.*, p. 49. The formula for calculating the 'conventional' measure is as follows:

$$D(1) = \frac{(E_t - E_{t-1})}{E_{t-1}} - \frac{(W_t - W_{t-1})}{W_{t-1}} \, 100$$

Where D(1) = drift
E = average weekly earnings
W = industry basic rate
t = one year.

6. *ibid.*, p. 50. See also NBPI Report No. 65 (Supplement), *Payments by Results Systems* (London: HMSO, 1969), pp. 20-25.
The formula for calculating the 'NBPI' measure is as follows:

$$D(2) = \frac{(E_t - W_t) - (E_{t-1} - W_{t-1})}{E_{t-1}} \, 100$$

The notation is the same as before, except that average weekly earnings exclude the cost of living bonus.

Street a measure of drift must take into account 'the automatic impact of the basic rate changes on all existing wage components under existing procedures including not only basic pay but also overtime and bonuses, plus rates, etc. which by local agreement or at management's discretion are basic rates linked'.[7] The reason is that with the exception of the cost of living bonus, increases in the industry basic rates multiply most of the other components by the same percentage;[8] to quote an example, a 5% increase in the industry rates is roughly equivalent to the same percentage increase in earnings. So the measure in Table 4.6, labelled the 'Fleet Street' measure to distinguish it from the other two, assumes that increases in the industry basic rates multiply the other components by the same percentage amount. The results are closer to those of the 'conventional' measure than the 'NBPI' but do little to alter the conclusion already reached about the significance of the components negotiated by the managements and chapels.

A possibility which must also be considered here is that the extent of drift was greater in those years in which increases in the industry basic rates were small or non-existent. The picture which emerges from comparing the three periods is confusing. In a number of offices the proportion of the increases in earnings resulting from increases in the components negotiated by the managements and chapels was greatest in the period 1964 to 1967, which had the smallest increase in industry basic rates. However, it would be wrong to exaggerate this finding. Figure 3.1 has already shown that there were considerable differences in the changes in earnings between the three periods. Furthermore, the increases in earnings were substantially less in the period 1964 to 1967 than the other two periods, with even reductions in earnings in some offices.

7. S. Lerner *et al.*, *Workshop Wage Determination* (Oxford: Pergamon, 1969), p. 20.
8. The formula for calculating the 'Fleet Street' measure is as follows:

$$D(3) = \frac{(E_t - E_{t-1}(\frac{W_t}{W_{t-1}})}{E_t - 1} \, 100$$

The notation is the same as before, except that average weekly earnings exclude the cost of living bonus.

TABLE 4.4

AVERAGE ANNUAL WAGE DRIFT, 1961:4: ALL OFFICES, SELECTED OCCUPATIONS (Proportion of increases in average weekly earnings resulting from differences and changes in components of pay negotiated by managements and chapels shown in brackets.)

Occupation	Conventional Measure		NBPI Measure		Fleet Street Measure	
Permanent Time Hands	3.2	(41.1)	4.7	(59.4)	2.9	(37.2)
Readers	7.2	(60.7)	8.1	(68.7)	6.2	(52.3)
Copyreaders	6.4	(55.3)	8.0	(68.6)	6.1	(52.8)
Process Workers	1.9	(29.4)	3.9	(59.0)	1.6	(24.7)
Stereotypers	1.4	(23.0)	4.2	(67.6)	1.1	(18.3)
Machine Managers	3.7	(43.9)	5.7	(72.0)	3.5	(41.5)
General Assistants	2.8	(34.9)	5.6	(70.8)	2.5	(31.2)
Publishing: Indoor	4.7	(48.3)	7.1	(72.0)	3.0	(31.1)
Engineers	1.5	(17.6)	2.6	(30.8)	−3.0	(—)
Electricians	1.1	(11.7)	2.8	(30.9)	−1.1	(—)

TABLE 4.5
AVERAGE ANNUAL WAGE DRIFT, 1964-7: ALL OFFICES, SELECTED OCCUPATIONS (Proportion of increases in average weekly earnings resulting from differences and changes in components of pay negotiated by managements and chapels shown in brackets.)

Occupation	Conventional Measure		NBPI Measure		Fleet Street Measure	
Permanent Time Hands	4.8	(76.3)	5.4	(84.8)	3.7	(58.2)
Readers	1.6	(51.1)	2.6	(67.2)	1.3	(43.8)
Copyreaders	3.4	(60.8)	4.2	(75.4)	3.2	(57.5)
Process Workers	−0.1	(—)	0.3	(19.6)	−0.5	(—)
Stereotypers	−0.3	(—)	0.6	(41.9)	−0.6	(—)
Machine Managers	−0.6	(—)	−0.03	(—)	−0.9	(—)
General Assistants	−1.3	(—)	−0.8	(—)	−2.1	(—)
Publishing: Indoor	1.1	(33.1)	2.0	(64.3)	0.8	(24.4)
Engineers	10.5	(82.9)	11.4	(89.9)	10.5	(82.9)
Electricians	8.5	(79.6)	8.8	(83.0)	7.7	(72.6)

TABLE 4.6
AVERAGE ANNUAL WAGE DRIFT, 1967-70: ALL OFFICES
SELECTED OCCUPATIONS (Proportion of increases in average weekly
earnings resulting from differences and changes in components of pay
negotiated by managements and chapels shown in brackets.)

Occupation	Conventional Measure		NBPI Measure		Fleet Street Measure	
Permanent Time Hands	8.3	(60.4)	11.0	(80.0)	8.6	(62.8)
Readers	10.0	(64.7)	12.5	(81.3)	10.3	(66.8)
Copyreaders	9.0	(59.2)	12.2	(89.1)	11.0	(79.9)
Process Workers	4.0	(42.7)	6.7	(71.6)	4.3	(46.6)
Stereotypers	2.9	(33.7)	6.5	(76.0)	3.2	(37.9)
Machine Managers	6.8	(55.0)	9.9	(80.7)	7.1	(58.0)
General Assistants	7.0	(52.8)	10.7	(81.3)	7.4	(56.0)
Publishing: Indoor	2.9	(31.6)	6.6	(72.3)	3.2	(35.0)
Engineers	6.2	(65.8)	7.9	(84.3)	6.1	(65.8)
Electricians	13.9	(81.3)	15.3	(89.5)	12.8	(80.6)

This, then, completes the description of the pay structure in the ten newspaper offices. To summarize, the main features which would seem to require explanation are: the differences in earnings between offices; the similarities in the size of the occupational earnings differentials, and the narrowing in these differentials; the changes in earnings by office and occupation; and the large number and variety of components of pay.

Part 2
The Analysis

Chapter 5

The Work Situation

Recent studies have suggested a number of variables in the work situation which might be significant for the findings in Chapters 2, 3, and 4.[1] The location[2] and size[3] of the newspaper offices might be significant factors in the differences in earnings between offices described in Chapter 2; so too might differences in the manufacturing process and the composition of the labour force.[4] The location and size of work groups in the manufacturing process might be significant for the size of occupational earnings differentials and the changes in earnings described in Chapter 3.[5] Other variables which might be significant are the frequency of discontinuities in production, the introduction of new technology, and the patterns of working.

Location of the Newspaper Offices

It might be thought that there would be an important relationship between the differences in earnings noted in Chapter 2 and the location of the newspaper offices. Not only were all the newspapers

1. For a review of these studies, see A. Fox, *Industrial Sociology and Industrial Relations*, Royal Commission Research Paper No. 3 (London: HMSO, 1966).
2. For a discussion of the significance of location, see S. Lerner *et al., Workshop Wage Determination* (Oxford: Pergamon, 1969), p. 68.
3. S. Lerner *et al.* found that 'in many sections of the engineering industry, there was a clear relationship between size of enterprise and size of earnings with larger enterprises having higher earnings'. *ibid.*, p. 32.
4. See, for example, J. Woodward, *Industrial Organisation: Theory and Practice* (London: Oxford University Press, 1965).
5. For a discussion of the significance of the size and location of work groups, see J. Kuhn, *Bargaining in Grievance Settlement* (New York: Columbia University Press, 1961); and L. R. Sayles, *Behaviour of Industrial Work Groups* (New York: J. Wiley, 1958).

53

printed at establishments situated within a radius of one mile from a point mid-way along Fleet Street, a number were printed at the same establishment. For example, the *Daily Mail* and *Evening News* are printed on the same presses, albeit at different times. During the period, these two newspapers also shared a number of maintenance and service facilities with the *Daily Sketch*, which was printed in an adjacent building. The *Guardian* was printed at the same establishment as the *Sunday Times* and shares maintenance and other service facilities. Finally, the *Observer* was printed under contract at the same establishment as *The Times* by production and maintenance workers who were employees of Thomson Organization Ltd.

No common patterns emerged, however, when the earnings of workers on newspapers printed at the same establishment were compared. The earnings of workers on the *Daily Sketch* and *Daily Mail* were no more similar than those of workers on the other popular newspapers. Even more significant was the fact that workers in some occupations on the *Evening News* had higher earnings than their counterparts on either of the daily newspapers. There were no common patterns between the *Guardian* and the *Sunday Times* or between the *Observer* and *The Times*, though few comparisons between a daily and a 'Sunday only' office are direct.

Technology of Production

The technology involved in manufacturing a newspaper is a special case of unit production.[6] Monday's newspaper is different from Tuesday's, Tuesday's different from Wednesday's, and so on. Then there is the time cycle. The printing of a newspaper takes place within specified time limits; at the one end the constraint is set by the need to include late news and at the other by the deadlines imposed by British Rail, the air agencies, and the wholesalers. The same is true of a Sunday newspaper, the only difference being the time scale. As one newspaper group put it in its guide issued to members of the public: 'Every newspaper has the same basic job to do. It must gather the news, sell advertising space, print it all quickly, publish, distribute, and sell copies.'[7] In other words, there

6. For a discussion of the different forms of technology, see Woodward, *op. cit.*
7. *A Great Newspaper . . . and Why*, issued by Beaverbrook Newspapers Ltd.

54

is nothing intrinsically different about the basic technology of the newspaper offices which would help to explain the findings in Chapters 2, 3, and 4. However, differences of detail might be significant.

There are no fundamental differences in the manufacturing process which would help to explain these findings. As the third section of Chapter I has described, the newspapers included in this study are printed by the same process, that is, letterpress, in which the image to be printed stands out as a raised surface on type or blocks.[8] They are then mass-produced on rotary press machines, with the plates bearing the image fastened to revolving cylinders, and the machines are fed with a continuous reel, or web, of newsprint.

The size of the offices does not seem to be significant either. Table 5.1 gives details of the numbers employed in the production and maintenance departments in 1961, 1964, 1967 and 1970, together with the correlation coefficients obtained by correlating these numbers with the earnings of 'All Occupations' in each office. The correlation coefficients suggest a negative association between size and earnings in three of the years, i.e. the smaller the size the higher the earnings, but they are not significant at the 5% level.

It is tempting to attribute the negative association between size and earnings to the composition of the labour force in the different offices. Table 5.2, which gives details of the number employed in each occupation in the production and maintenance departments, confirms that the offices with the smaller total labour force employ more workers in the occupations which have higher industry basic rates, or more Linotype Operators and Piece Case Hands who are paid by results. However, this line of argument breaks down when the offices with the larger total labour force are examined more closely. In some, Linotype Operators and Piece Case Hands and other occupations with the higher industry basic rates were lower in the rank orders of earnings.

Table 5.2 confirms that size of department had some significance for the difference between the offices noted above. In the offices with the smaller total labour force the proportion of workers in the

8. For brief details of the main printing processes, see *Report of a Court of Inquiry into the problems caused by the introduction of web-offset machines into the printing industry, and the problems arising from the introduction of other modern printing techniques and the arrangements which should be adopted within the industry for dealing with them*, Cmnd. 3184 (London: HMSO, 1967).

TABLE 5.1
TOTAL NUMBER EMPLOYED IN THE PRODUCTION AND MAINTENANCE DEPARTMENTS

Office No.	1961	1964	1967	1970
Q	205	227	217	212
R	278	321	337	359
S	424	436	432	426
T	472	484	555	596
U	913	850	854	880
V	981	1171	1118	1078
W	1124	1086	1030	823
X	1165	1286	1154	1091
Y	1768	1750	1697	1451
Z	1799	1808	1697	1609
Correlation Coefficient (Total number employed and Earnings of 'All Occupations')	—.1033	+.0079	—.4398	—.3121

occupations in the composing and reading departments, for example, was greater than in the offices with the larger total labour force. In the latter, on the other hand, the proportion of workers in the occupations in the machine and publishing departments was greater. However, it would be wrong to exaggerate the significance of size of department. Engineers and Electricians were relatively few in number in most offices and yet they were amongst the highest-paid occupations and also enjoyed above-average increases in earnings.

It is true that most occupations requiring an apprenticeship qualification were amongst the highest-paid occupations.[9] Beyond this, however, the possession of such a qualification does not seem to be significant. Both Chapters 2 and 3 have produced evidence to show that the department was the distinguishing characteristic; the dispersion of earnings was similar among occupations in the same department and so too were the changes in earnings.

9. The amount of skill required for many of the jobs in Fleet Street which need an apprenticeship qualification is a controversial issue. The EIU Report doubted whether any of the jobs in the production departments needed more than one year's training. The NGA, on the other hand, has claimed that its members are trained to perform a range of activities which will equip them for employment elsewhere in the industry in the event of redundancy.

56

Since the similarities between occupations in the same department are the subject of more detailed examination in Chapter 8, it remains to be seen if differences in the manufacturing process from department to department will help to explain the findings in Chapters 2 and 3. The distinction between occupations involved in individual and group activities does not seem to be significant. Some of the occupations involved in individual activities such as Linotype Operators and Piece Case Hands were amongst the highest-paid occupations, and yet the increases in earnings of these occupations were below average in most offices. Revisers and Linotype Assistants, on the other hand, were relatively low in the rank orders of occupational earnings but enjoyed above-average increases in earnings. The occupations involved in group activities in the machine and publishing departments were relatively high in the rank orders of occupational earnings but received below-average increases in earnings.

The distinction between occupations involved in the manufacture of the 'first copy'[10] and those involved in its mass production does not seem to be significant either. Of the occupations involved in the manufacture of the 'first copy', Permanent Time Hands and Proofpullers received above-average increases in earnings whereas Linotype Operators and Piece Case Hands received below-average increases. Furthermore, the increases in earnings of the occupations in the machine and publishing departments were below average, and yet these occupations were directly affected by the page size of the newspapers and the number of copies produced.

The location of Engineers and Electricians in the manufacturing process might help to explain why these occupations were amongst the highest paid in most offices and why they enjoyed above-average increases in earnings. Maintenance workers work throughout the newspaper offices in ones and twos and small groups. Changes, especially technological ones, taking place in any of the production departments usually have some impact on them. The position of Process Workers might also help to explain why they were lower in the rank orders of occupational earnings than in the rank order of industry basic rates in most offices, and why they received below-average increases in earnings. SLADE is the only trade union whose members in Fleet Street are unable to stop production totally

10. See the third section of Chapter 1 for a simple definition of 'first copy'.

TABLE 5.2

NUMBERS EMPLOYED IN OCCUPATIONS/DEPARTMENTS: OCTOBER 1967
(Proportions shown in brackets)

Occupation	Office									
	Q	R	S	T	U	V	W	X	Y	Z
Wireroom Operators	5(2.3)	—	—	—	—	18(1.6)	17(1.7)	27(2.3)	—	14(0.8)
Telephoto Operators	5(2.3)	—	—	—	—	2(0.2)	14(1.3)	12(1.0)	—	8(0.5)
Photoprinters	—	—	9(2.1)	4(0.7)	3(0.4)	3(0.3)	10(1.0)	2(0.2)	6(0.4)	12(0.7)
Permanent Time Hands	21(9.7)	50(14.8)	35(8.1)	60(10.8)	41(4.8)	71(6.4)	35(3.4)	90(7.8)	53(3.1)	48(2.8)
Linotype Operators	23(10.6)	50(14.8)	26(6.0)	40(7.2)	52(6.1)	68(6.1)	38(3.7)	51(4.4)	55(3.2)	39(2.3)
Piece Case Hands	5(2.3)	22(6.5)	16(3.7)	17(3.1)	17(2.0)	19(1.7)	25(2.4)	42(3.6)	32(1.9)	30(1.8)
Proof Pullers	2(1.1)	9(2.7)	6(1.4)	21(3.8)	8(0.9)	16(1.4)	8(0.8)	15(1.3)	9(0.5)	10(0.6)
Linotype Assistants	4(2.2)	5(1.5)	7(1.6)	5(0.9)	6(0.7)	6(0.5)	9(0.9)	9(0.8)	15(0.9)	9(0.5)
Readers	14(6.4)	28(8.3)	16(3.7)	30(5.4)	23(2.7)	44(4.0)	21(2.0)	38(3.3)	31(1.8)	23(1.4)
Revisers	2(1.1)	9(2.7)	3(0.7)	10(1.8)	4(0.5)	13(1.2)	11(1.1)	8(0.7)	10(0.6)	8(0.5)
Copyreaders	18(8.3)	28(8.3)	17(3.9)	34(6.1)	24(2.8)	47(4.2)	24(2.3)	36(3.1)	35(2.1)	22(1.3)
Process Workers	—	11(3.3)	31(7.2)	25(4.5)	34(4.0)	39(3.4)	56(5.4)	53(4.6)	—	54(3.2)
Stereotypers	18(8.3)	24(7.1)	24(5.6)	30(5.4)	49(5.7)	55(4.9)	52(5.0)	69(6.0)	137(8.1)	79(4.7)

Machine Managers	7(3.2)	9(2.7)	21(4.9)	14(2.5)	40(4.7)	48(4.3)	30(2.9)	68(5.9)	76(4.5)	130(7.7)
Brake Hands	4(2.2)	6(1.8)	14(3.2)	8(1.4)	18(2.1)	32(2.8)	46(4.5)	46(4.0)	42(2.5)	135(8.0)
Magazine Hands	7(3.2)	13(3.9)	35(8.1)	6(1.1)	34(4.0)	63(5.6)	40(3.8)	56(4.9)	48(2.8)	207(12.2)
Oilers	12(5.5)	6(1.8)	34(7.9)	13(2.3)	52(6.1)	106(9.5)	82(8.0)	88(7.6)	174(10.3)	160(9.4)
General Assistants	17(7.8)	22(6.5)	35(8.1)	36(6.5)	104(12.2)	234(20.9)	108(10.3)	234(20.3)	288(17.0)	126(7.4)
Publishing: Indoor	37(17.1)	31(9.2)	82(19.0)	112(20.2)	121(14.1)	155(13.9)	123(11.9)	147(12.7)	89(5.2)	381(22.5)
Publishing: Outdoor	14(6.4)	—	11(2.5)	12(2.2)	145(17.0)	17(1.5)	18(1.7)	27(2.3)	376(22.2)	—
Engineers	—	5(1.5)	—	10(1.8)	9(1.1)	11(1.0)	59(5.7)	9(0.8)	7(0.4)	38(2.2)
Engineers' Asstnts	—	4(1.2)	—	8(1.4)	9(1.1)	—	17(1.7)	7(0.6)	101(6.0)	—
Electricians	—	7(2.1)	—	10(1.8)	8(0.9)	9(0.8)	18(1.7)	27(2.3)	16(0.9)	81(4.8)
Electricians' Asstnts	—	7(2.1)	—	1(0.2)	7(0.8)	3(0.3)	18(1.7)	—	22(1.3)	—
Messengers/Doormen	2(1.1)	—	10(2.3)	49(8.8)	46(5.4)	39(3.4)	·91(8.8)	—	75(4.4)	—
Cleaners/Firemen										
All Occupations	217	337	432	555	854	1118	1030	1154	1697	1697

by taking industrial action.[11]

Otherwise there is no evidence to suggest that location in the manufacturing process was significant. Because of the many changes in the product and the fluctuations in the level of activity in the product market, discontinuities in production are extremely frequent in every department. Indeed, there can be few industries in which discontinuities in production are so many and varied. As stated above, each issue of the newspaper is a different product. Then there are a number of editions in each issue, a number of page changes in each edition, and so on.

Although Fleet Street is not noted for its technological innovations,[12] it does seem that some technological changes were significant. In one office, for example, the exceptionally high earnings of Wireroom Operators are explained by the fact they were working with teletype-setting equipment. In another, the marked increase in the earnings of Linotype Operators is explained by the introduction of computer type-setting. However, the mechanization of the publishing departments, involving a change from manual to automated methods in handling newspapers, seems to have had limited significance, since increases in earnings in the publishing department were not exceptionally large.

Patterns of Working

It might also be thought that the extremely complex patterns of working in the production and maintenance departments would be significant.[13] The daily and evening newspapers usually require workers in the production departments on five nights/days out of six, and workers in the maintenance and service departments, such as the process department five nights/days out of seven. They also require workers involved in the manufacture of the 'first copy' on two, and sometimes three, shifts in each twenty-four-hour cycle — a

11. SLADE discovered this to its cost in 1968. See Appendix II.
12. The price of trade union co-operation is not the only reason. The fact is that the existing technology has stood the test of time remarkably well. For brief details of recent technological innovations in printing, see *Report of a Court of Inquiry* etc., *op. cit.*, pp. 48 and 49.
13. In 1967, for example, 1207 production workers regularly worked four shifts each week, 919 worked three shifts, 179 worked two shifts, and 4319 worked one shift. These details do not include non-regular shifts.

requirement which extends to workers in the maintenance and service departments. Workers in the occupations in the machine and publishing departments, on the other hand, are only required for the mass production stage, starting work on the daily newspapers between 21.00 and 22.00 hours and finishing at about 4.30 hours.

The distinction between day and night work does not seem to be significant. It is true that workers on the production shifts of the daily newspapers who work at night earned more than those on non-production shifts who work during the day. But then workers on the production shifts of the evening newspapers who work during the day earned more than those on non-production shifts who work at night. It might be thought that workers on production shifts on the daily newspapers who work at night would earn more than those on production shifts on the evening newspapers who work during the day. However, this was not necessarily so, as the first section of this chapter has already pointed out in the case of the *Evening News*.

The distinction between workers involved in one shift in each twenty-four-hour cycle, such as those in occupations in the machine and publishing departments, and those involved in more than one does not seem to be significant either. Of those in the latter category, Process Workers, for example, were in the middle of the rank orders of occupational earnings and had lower than average increases in earnings, while Engineers and Electricians were towards the top of the rank orders and had above-average increases in earnings.

The patterns of working in the 'dual' offices (the *Daily Express* and *Sunday Express*, the *Daily Mirror* and *Sunday Mirror*, and the *Daily Telegraph* and *Sunday Telegraph*) seem to be significant in one respect. Occupations in the machine department, which work four shifts on the daily newspaper and one on the Sunday newspaper earned more than their counterparts in the machine departments of the 'morning only' offices which were close competitors. Otherwise, the patterns of working in the 'dual' offices do not seem to have been significant.

This chapter has been unable to find a significant relationship between the differences in earnings noted in Chapter 2 and the location of the newspaper offices. It has suggested that there might be some relationship between the rank orders of earnings and the changes in earnings noted in Chapter 3 and the introduction of new technology; that the location of maintenance and Process workers in

61

the manufacturing process might be significant; and that size of department might also have some influence. Otherwise, this chapter has been negative in its conclusions. However, most empirical studies of pay structure have looked to the labour market for explanations. So the labour market is the subject of the chapter which follows.

Chapter 6

The Labour Market

The labour market is held to influence pay structure through the interaction of the supply of and demand for labour. In the words of MacKay and his colleagues: 'traditional labour market theory predicts that competition between employers for the labour available, and economic rationality on the part of employees, will set in train forces which tend to equate the net advantages offered by different employments'.[1] It follows that the differences and changes in earnings described in Chapters 2 and 3 must be 'compensating' or 'real'.[2] If the managements compete for labour and workers are unrestricted in their mobility, these differentials might compensate for differences in the other qualities of the job: workers might have to satisfy more rigorous hiring standards or undergo a more lengthy period of training. If, on the other hand, competition and mobility are restricted, these differentials might be settled with little regard for supply and demand conditions in the labour market.[3]

1 D. I. MacKay *et al., Labour Markets Under Different Employment Conditions* (London: Allen and Unwin, 1971), p. 65.
2. S. Rottenberg, 'On Choice in Labor Markets'. *Industrial and Labor Relations Review* (January 1956), p. 185.
3. In the case of inter-plant differentials MacKay and his colleagues (*op. cit.*, pp. 22-3) suggest that it is possible to establish: '. . . two contrasting hypotheses . . . If wages are not a key factor in job choice there will be little relationship between plant level wages. In the extreme case the supply of labour would be price-elastic and there would be no tendency for a common level of wages to be established. Labour turnover would not be responsive to differences or changes in relative earnings. Wage-setting would depend on the administrative decision of management influenced by union pressure but unaffected by mobility or potential mobility in the labour market. Alternatively, if labour is responsive to wage differentials the plant's wage policy will be influenced by the actions of its competitors and by its experience in recruiting and retaining labour.'

Characteristics of the Labour Force

Lack of an appropriate measure makes it impossible to compare their quality, but age and length of employment distributions of workers in the production departments suggest that the labour force in the different offices is relatively homogeneous. Details of the age distribution in the production departments given in Table 6.1 may be compared with those, in Table 6.2, of workers in 'All Industries' and in 'Mining and Quarrying', a group with one of the oldest labour forces. The comparison suggests that the number of workers in the production departments in Fleet Street over the age of forty is amongst the highest of all the industries in the SIC Orders.[4] At the other end of the age range, there are very few workers in the production department in Fleet Street under the age of twenty-four. If the number of these workers with less than five years' employment

TABLE 6.1

AGE DISTRIBUTIONS OF PRODUCTION WORKERS: 1967

Occupation/Department	Total Number	Percentage Aged		
		—24	25-40	41+
Press Telegraphists	188	1.6	39.4	59.0
Linotype Operators	651	0	29.3	70.7
Piece Case Hands	316	0	4.5	95.5
Permanent Time Hands	897	0.2	48.9	50.9
Readers	381	0.3	24.2	75.6
Stereotypers	689	3.5	37.3	59.2
Machine Managers	464	0.2	34.7	65.1
Process Workers	445	0.4	25.0	74.6
Photoprinters	134	15.7	39.6	44.8
Revisers and Copyreaders	504	11.1	39.9	49.0
Engineers and Linotype Assistants	521	1.0	21.0	78.0
Machine Assistants	2843	0.2	27.9	71.9
Publishing	2398	0.9	22.9	76.2
Proofpullers/Pressmen	156	2.6	27.6	69.9
Others	1405	1.8	16.9	81.3

Note: These details relate to the age of regular production workers employed five shifts in one newspaper office as at September 1967. No details of the age of maintenance workers are available. (Source: NPA)

4. One manager told the Royal Commission on the Press: 'They can go on as long as they can stand up in some unions.' Royal Commission on the Press, 1961-2, *Minutes of Oral Evidence*, Cmnd. 1812-4 (London: HMSO, 1962), para. 2663.

TABLE 6.2

AGE DISTRIBUTIONS: MINING & QUARRYING, ALL SIC INDUSTRIES
JUNE 1967

	Total Aged			
	—20	20-39	40-64	60+
Mining and Quarrying	6%	32%	62%	10%
All Industries and Services	9%	41%	47%	3%

(Source: *Employment and Productivity Gazette*, June 1968, p. 47.)

TABLE 6.3

LENGTH OF EMPLOYMENT DISTRIBUTIONS OF
PRODUCTION WORKERS: 1967

Occupation/Department	Total Number	Percentage with Years of Service		
		—5	6-20	21+
Press Telegraphists	188	3.4	33.4	28.2
Linotype Operators	651	20.3	61.8	26.4
Piece Case Hands	316	0.6	53.2	46.8
Permanent Time Hands	897	33.9	57.4	8.7
Readers	381	39.4	47.7	12.5
Stereotypers	689	26.3	58.6	15.1
Machine Managers	464	28.4	63.6	8.4
Process Workers	445	20.6	63.6	15.7
Photoprinters	134	35.0	47.0	17.9
Revisers and Copyreaders	504	45.4	42.5	12.1
Engineers and Linotype Assistants	521	23.8	62.9	13.4
Machine Assistants	2843	22.8	53.6	23.6
Publishing	2398	4.7	75.1	20.3
Proofpullers/Pressmen	156	25.6	54.5	21.2
Others	1405	37.9	51.6	10.5

Note: These details relate to the length of employment of regular production workers
employed five shifts in one newspaper office as at September 1967. No
details are available in the case of maintenance workers. (Source: NPA)

is taken into account (see Table 6.3), it can be supposed that most recruits start employment in Fleet Street at a relatively advanced age. The details of the length of employment distribution in Table 6.3 also suggest that the majority of workers are long-term employees of the newspapers.[5] *Ad hoc* inquiries by the NPA into labour turnover support this conclusion: the annual separation is low, and the main reasons for terminating employment are death and retirement. There is no evidence, therefore, to suggest a significant relationship between the differences in earnings noted in Chapter 2 and the characteristics of the labour force in the different offices.

Job Entry Controls

In most empirical studies of pay structure it has proved difficult to determine whether or not differentials like those described in Chapters 2 and 3 are the result of the interaction of supply and demand conditions in the labour market.[6] In Fleet Street this question can only be answered by studying the effect of the job entry controls described in this section. To do this, it will be helpful to distinguish between entry to 'regular' and to 'casual' jobs. The job entry controls in the case of 'regular' jobs are to be found in slightly different forms in all the production and maintenance departments. The job entry controls in the case of 'casual' jobs are to be found mainly in the machine and publishing departments, although there is a limited amount of casual working in some other departments.

---

5. There was an especially large influx in the period following the ending of newsprint rationing and the increases in page size in 1956. See Chapter 7. A Government Social Survey published in 1966 found that only 6% of skilled and partly skilled manual workers had more than twenty years in the same job. Only 4% of unskilled workers had more than twenty years in the same job. See R. Clausen and A. I. Harris, *Labour Mobility in Great Britain, 1953-63* (London: HMSO, 1966).
6. For example, MacKay *et al.* (*op. cit.*, p. 65) have written: 'This is the nub of the difficulty which faces all applied research in labour economics. Labour market theory is so versatile, it admits of so many possible influences which may be important in job choice, that it is possible to rationalise almost any set of observed events.'

The method of filling vacancies differs from department to department. In many the overseer or FOC simply notifies the appropriate branch. The branch then sends an applicant. If the overseer is satisfied, he hires him. If not, he asks the branch to send another applicant, and so the process continues. On the face of it, the power of the veto seems to rest with the overseer, but this is very much a question of degree. In practice managers have very little discretion over these hiring arrangements. The knowledge that the rejection of an applicant only starts the process off again tends to restrain the exercise of the veto: it makes for an easy life to accept the first applicant. One manager told the Royal Commission on Trade Unions: 'We are of course perfectly entitled to reject anybody the union sends. But if we go on rejecting people, eventually we just do not get anybody at all.'[7] It is important to note that the managements do not have the option of leaving the vacancy unfilled. Manning levels are negotiated by the NPA and the trade unions or the managements and chapels. It is also the usual practice for workers who leave to be replaced automatically; the only exceptions are by agreement between the management and the chapel.

There are some interesting variations in the composing department. Vacancies for Linotype Operators and Permanent Time Hands are often filled by members of the NGA who have worked in the office as holiday reliefs. Names of likely applicants are taken by the overseer or the FOC, and they may be offered a full-time job when a vacancy occurs. The freedom of choice of the Printer, or composing department manager, is more limited, however, in the case of vacancies among Piece Case Hands. These are filled by promotion from the Permanent Time Hands who have enforced the principle that this promotion should be determined by seniority — hence the age and length of employment of Piece Case Hands shown in Tables 6.1 and 6.3.[8]

The situation in the reading department is unique. The Reviser and Copyreader, who are members of NATSOPA, may apply to

7. Royal Commission on Trade Unions and Employers' Associations, *Minutes of Evidence*, 59 (London: HMSO, 1967), Question 9342.
8. In answer to the question: 'Is piece work a natural progression for the chap who is on time?' an official of the LTS replied: 'It is for 90%. Promotion from time to piece is by seniority.' Royal Commission on the Press, 1961-2, *Minutes of Oral Evidence, loc. cit.*, Vol. 2, para. 9541.

take the Readers' examination which is organized by the NGA. If they are successful, they may be accepted as Readers and their membership transferred to the NGA when the number of existing members falls short of requirements. However, the newly promoted Reader is not allowed to start work immediately in Fleet Street; he must work in the printing industry for a minimum period of two years before he is allowed to apply to the London Region of the NGA for a vacancy in Fleet Street.

The overseer is hardly ever involved in filling vacancies among members of NATSOPA in the machine department. Vacancies among the different grades are filled from the grade below according to seniority by the chapel. Vacancies among the most junior grade, General Assistant, are either notified to the branch or are filled by recruitment from the 'regular' casuals.[9] Vacancies are filled in the same way in the publishing department from members of SOGAT. Vacancies among Engineers and Electricians are usually notified to the appropriate branch. In both cases there is an understanding that the branch will have an opportunity to submit applicants from their register. Vacancies among Electricians are sometimes filled by the promotion of Electricians' Assistants who are members of the same union. There are no similar promotion prospects for Engineers' Assistants who are members of NATSOPA.

In some of the departments in which the RIRMA branch of NATSOPA has its members, vacancies among Linotype and Engineers' Assistants are often filled by promotion from within the office. In this case it is likely that there will be informal discussions between the management and branch officers.

Note that very few regular jobs are filled from within the internal labour market[10] by apprenticeship.[11] Since 1967 no apprentices have

9. Casual working is discussed later in this section.
10. MacKay *et al.* (*op. cit.*, p. 31) suggest that: 'The labour market internal to a plant can take two extreme forms. A closed or structured market is one in which present employees get favoured treatment. New workers are only recruited at the lowest grade and all other vacancies which arise are filled by internal promotion. In contrast an open or unstructured market is one in which there is a port of entry for every grade of work so that a vacancy is filled by external recruitment rather than by internal mobility.' See also C. Kerr, 'The Balkanisation of Labour Markets', in E. W. Bakke (ed.), *Labour Mobility and Economic Opportunity* (Cambridge: Massachusetts Institute of Technology Press, 1954); and P. B. Doeringer and M. J. Piore, *Internal Labour Markets and Manpower Analysis* (Lexington: D. C. Heath, 1971).
11. Many of the occupations in the production and maintenance departments require an apprenticeship qualification. In the great majority of cases this is

been engaged in the departments in which the NGA and SLADE have their members. Before 1967 the number of apprentices was small and they were restricted to the foundry. Agreements between the NPA and the LSC and PMMTS had simply stated that there should be no apprentices in the composing and machine departments. There were agreements between the NPA and SLADE and the NSES providing for the engagement of apprentices, but these were terminated in 1960 and 1967 respectively. The only departments in which apprentices were engaged in 1970 were the photographic and electrical departments, and they were very few in number.

In short, the trade unions are the sole or main source of the supply of labour. Using the terminology developed by McCarthy, there is a labour supply closed shop;[12] by implication there is also a pre-entry closed shop since the worker has to be a member of the appropriate union before he can be engaged. The result is that very few regular jobs are filled from within the internal labour market by promotion. Jobs lie within the jurisdiction of the different unions and the demarcation between them is jealously guarded.

So far this section has described the job entry controls as they affect the relationship between the vacancy and the trade union. Equally significant is the relationship between the trade union and the member who applies for a vacancy. The unions have had to pay attention to this relationship for two reasons. First, the members have come to look upon the union as a labour exchange;[13] the member who is out of work or wishes to change his job goes automatically to the branch. Second, there is competition among the members for jobs in Fleet Street because of the levels of earnings. Given these pressures, the unions have found it necessary to devise

---

completed in the printing industry, where the BFMP operates apprenticeship schemes jointly with the printing unions.

12. W. E. J. McCarthy, *The Closed Shop in Britain* (Oxford: Blackwell, 1964). In fact, he uses Fleet Street to illustrate the labour supply closed shop.

13. For many years the printing unions were recognized as labour exchanges by the Ministry of Labour. The NSES, for example, told the Royal Commission on the Press, 1961-2, that: 'During the depression, the war, and during the operation of the Control of Engagements Order the unions were appointed employment agencies for their own members by the Ministry of Labour.' Royal Commission on the Press, 1961-2, *Documentary Evidence, loc. cit.*, Vol. 4, p. 87. See also E. Howe and H. E. Waite, *The London Society of Compositors* (London: Cassell, 1948); and A. E. Musson, *The Typographical Association* (London: Oxford University Press, 1954).

regulations which ensure fair treatment in the filling of vacancies in Fleet Street.[14]

The regulations are similar in most of the branches. A member who wants a regular job in Fleet Street puts his name on a register at the branch; he then receives notice of a vacancy according to his seniority on the register. Some branches also ensure fair treatment with more specific regulations. As noted above, NGA insists that a member works for at least two years in the printing industry after completing his apprenticeship before he applies for a vacancy in Fleet Street. SLADE has greater control generally because of the so-called 'white card' system. A member wishing to apply for a vacancy must first obtain a white card from the branch. Only one white card is issued in respect of each vacancy and a member who does not have the card is not allowed to apply.

The most significant result of these regulations is that it is extremely rare for any of the trade unions to allow a member who already has a job in Fleet Street to move from one office to another. As one union explained to the Royal Commission on the Press, 1961-2:

The union does retain control of transfer from one job to another within the industry or otherwise, where employers are of their own free will and accord paying higher wages or higher extras than other employers, we would rapidly find the queue outside the door, and other people who could not, for one reason or another, afford to pay, being denuded of staff.[15]

In other words, workers in the production and maintenance departments are unable to respond to differences and changes in the relative levels of pay by moving from office to office and from occupation to occupation. The member does not get a regular job until he is relatively old and, having got one, tends to stay in it — which explains the age and length of employment distributions described in the previous section.

How did these job entry controls come about? Most of the controls described above had emerged in one form or another by 1939 and the origins, to quote the evidence of one trade union to the Royal

14. M. W. Reder has written: '. . . union entry restrictions and job allocations are not peculiar to manualists, as Perlman thought, but are manifestations of the ethics of the queue which are accepted throughout most of the community.' 'Job Scarcity and the Nature of Union Power', *Industrial and Labor Relations Review* (1959), p. 35. The reference is to S. Perlman, *Theory of the Labor Movement* (New York: Macmillan, 1928).
15. Royal Commission on the Press, 1961-2, *Documentary Evidence, loc. cit.*, Vol. 1, p. 137.

Commission on the Press, 1961-2, are 'buried in antiquity'.[16] The aim of controlling and restricting entry, which was expressed in the requirement that each worker should have an apprenticeship qualification and that there should be a ratio of apprentices to journeymen, dates back to the earliest days of printing. These regulations were designed to protect master and journeymen alike from foreign and domestic competition, and were enforced for many years by the Stationers' Company with government support. Towards the end of the eighteenth century these regulations slowly disappeared under the pressure of changing attitudes to protection and an increase in the demand for printing. The small craft societies which developed among the journeymen struggled throughout the nineteenth century to fill the vacuum with their own regulations. They were not only anxious to deny the employer access to alternative supplies of labour and to expand the number of jobs but also to prevent other societies from encroaching on their preserve — hence job demarcation.

An equally important stage in the development of these controls has already been touched on earlier in this section. Once the members had come to look upon the union as a labour exchange and there was competition for jobs in Fleet Street, the unions found it necessary to devise regulations which ensured fair treatment in the filling of vacancies. The fact that jobs in Fleet Street are reserved for existing members is also the main reason for the lack of apprentices.

Over the years employers have acquiesced in the development of these controls. Originally the restrictions on entry were in their interest. Later they helped to take wages out of competition. They also took from employers the burden of recruitment, since it was convenient to rely on the FOC or the branch. Once the controls were established, it was difficult to do anything about them. As one manager confessed to the Royal Commission on Trade Unions, 'It is extraordinarily difficult to see how, the situation having developed as it is, we can recover it quickly — and what can we do? We are obligated to employ union members.'[17]

16. *ibid.*, Vol. 4, p. 137.
17. Royal Commission on Trade Unions and Employers' Associations, *Minutes of Evidence, loc. cit.*, Question 9346.

Table 6.4 gives some impression of the number of non-regular shifts worked by members of the machine branch of NATSOPA and the LCB of SOGAT, the two branches mainly affected. As in the case of regular jobs, the branch is the main source of the supply of labour to the large number of casual jobs in the machine and publishing departments. When the number of regulars on rota falls short of the agreed staffing level for the page size, the overseer or, in many

TABLE 6.4

AVERAGE NUMBER OF NON-REGULAR SHIFTS PER NIGHT:
APRIL 1968 — MARCH 1969

Month	Machine Department		Publishing Department	
	Daily	Sunday	Daily	Sunday
April	280	388	439	926
May	300	439	435	944
June	303	439	435	944
July	291	458	623	1115
August	309	343	522	993
September	327	489	531	1093
October	316	457	495	990
November	303	417	460	962
December	303	300	432	918
January	262	427	397	977
February	202	442	425	1016
March	225	425	515	1113
Average	286	423	490	1019

Note: These details include sixth nights worked by regulars and 'ghost' shifts. Given the inadequacy of the information available, it is extremely difficult to estimate the proportion of non-regular to regular shifts. Using the numbers of regular workers quoted earlier in this chapter as a base and making allowances for a five-day week, it would appear that in 1968-9 in the machine departments of the daily newspapers the proportion of non-regular shifts was of the order of 11%; in the publishing departments it was something like 17%. On the Sunday newspapers the proportions were much higher. Taking the machine and publishing departments together, it would appear that the proportion of non-regular shifts was about one third. In the case of the Sunday newspapers the base was the number of regular workers working one shift. (See note 13 to Chapter 5.)

offices, the FOC puts in a 'call' to the branch for casuals to make up the difference. Both the machine branch of NATSOPA and the LCB of SOGAT have a 'call' office with a clerk who directs the casuals to the offices requiring their services. The overseer has no power of veto in the case of casuals sent by the branch in this way; any complaints about their competence are usually made in general terms after the event.

In practice the situation is a little more complicated. In both branches there are two main categories of casual members: 'regular' casuals, known in the LCB of SOGAT as 'regular jobbing hands', and 'casual' casuals. The difference is as follows. The 'regular' casual has a fixed and regular pattern of appearances; he may, for example, work a Saturday night, the highest-paid night, and three or four nights in the week. The 'regular' casual enjoys most of the advantages of the regular worker, such as holidays and pensions, the only difference being that he does not work a full week in any one office. The 'casual' casual, on the other hand, does not have a fixed pattern of employment. He relies on the branch for notice of work, attending the 'call' office each night for direction. He usually receives the same earnings as the regular worker and the 'regular' casual, but none of the fringe benefits.

The importance of the 'Sunday only' newspapers in the operation of the casual system is revealed in the priorities which are accorded to the 'regular jobbing hand' in the LCB of SOGAT. The 'regular jobbing hand' is allowed to work 56 hours a week, Saturday night counting as 12 hours and week nights as 10 hours. He is not debarred from working as a 'casual' casual during the week providing he does not exceed the overall limit.

Many 'regular jobbing hands' were confirmed in these patterns of working as a result of a succession of decasualization agreements negotiated between the LCB of SOGAT and the NPA beginning in 1963. They then formed the nucleus of those who became known as '3 and 1' men, i.e. regulars who work Saturday night usually in a 'Sunday only' office and three nights during the week on a daily or evening newspaper.[18]

The situation is not dissimilar in the machine branch of

18. It is important to note that in the interests of the 'regular jobbing hand' the LCB of SOGAT does not allow 'dual' working on a daily and Sunday newspaper in the same office. Because of the smaller number of casuals involved, the machine branch of NATSOPA has not found it necessary to impose such a ban.

NATSOPA. Here too the 'Sunday only' offices are the key to understanding the patterns of working which have developed; workers who are regularly employed on Saturday night form a pool of labour seeking work throughout the week. In the machine branch of NATSOPA, however, there is no special category similar to the 'regular jobbing hand', though many individuals developed fixed patterns of employment during the week which were recognized in decasualization agreements negotiated between the Branch and the NPA beginning in 1966.

In the machine branch of NATSOPA, however, there are two categories of 'casual' casuals. There is a group variously described as the 'red toppers' or 'nomads' who have the priority in the claim on casual work because of their seniority. Usually they do not appear at the 'call' office but make application to the FOCs direct; some develop a pattern in one or two offices while others move from office to office depending on the earnings on the night. But the 'nomads' are the only group who are free from the direct control of the branch, which also keeps a very tight rein on the total number of members who are allowed to seek work in Fleet Street as casuals.

Further restrictions are imposed by the chapels which are able to manipulate the arrangements for ordering casuals to suit themselves. The FOC, for example, may keep his own list of casual members, offering work to 'regular' casuals already working in the office or to 'nomads' in the machine department. In the publishing department especially there is a high incidence of sixth-night working among the regular workers. Both branches are opposed in principle to sixth-night working but there is often a conflict between the regular and casual members about enforcing a ban; the LCB of SOGAT, for example, ruled an end to the practice in 1967, only to rescind this under pressure from the chapels in the newspaper offices whose members had become accustomed to the additional earnings. Finally, the FOC may simply put in a 'call' to the branch for fewer casuals than are required by the agreed staffing level which ensures that the management has to pay 'ghost' or 'shortage' monies to the chapel.[19] The casual worker, then, like the regular worker, is not an entirely free agent.

19. In its written evidence to the Royal Commission on the Press, the *Daily Telegraph* illustrates how the practices had developed in that office: 'This practice arose when the shortages were very small. On the assumption that some extra effort would be required by the rest of the men, the practice did not

Many of the job entry controls practised by NATSOPA and SOGAT bear a close resemblance to those of the craft societies and there can be little doubt that there was some imitation. However, in the machine and publishing departments these unions were faced with special problems. In the early years of mass production newspapers in Fleet Street, workers in these two departments found themselves in a predominantly casual labour market. The 'Sunday only' newspapers required the bulk of their labour force in these two departments on Saturday night only. Workers regularly employed on a Saturday night thus formed a pool of labour looking for work throughout the week. But the labour force was also predominantly casual on the daily and evening newspapers because of the fluctuations in the page sizes from issue to issue. Later, but before the negotiation of comprehensive agreements, the need to cover for holidays and sickness made a further contribution to the casual problem. In the beginning, then, the job entry controls which workers in the machine and publishing departments developed were designed to protect themselves against the worst abuses of casual employment. The fact that the 'Sunday only' newspapers still require the bulk of their labour force on Saturday night only and few of the daily and evening newspapers have sufficient regulars to cope with issues above the average page size also explains why they have not been relaxed. But these job entry controls were also a pre-condition of the union establshing itself as an effective organization. Unless the union was able to recruit *all* the workers in the casual pool on the understanding that it would find them work, it had little hope of protecting them against alternative supplies of labour.

---

seem very objectionable. However, over the years and particularly after the reduction of the working fortnight from eleven nights to ten, the figures of this 'ghosting' rose extravagantly. For example, the *Daily Telegraph* in the machine room on a 28pp., for which a staff of 306 has been agreed (though only after objection by the management), regularly runs 54 short a night and their supposed earnings are divided amongst those working, giving them about £1.25 per man.' It went on to explain that 'ghost' or 'shortage' money was paid in the publishing department because of lack of bench-space: 'A house agreement made at the beginning of the war laid down 50 parcels per man per night as a basis of staffing. Circulation has so risen that the numbers of men required by these terms cannot be accommodated on the benches. Because of the shortage, a payment of one hour's overtime on 16pp. and two hours' overtime on 18pp. and upwards is therefore made to all men actually working.' Royal Commission on the Press, 1961-2, *Documentary Evidence, loc. cit.*, Vol. 1, p. 166.

Employment Situation in the Printing Industry

It might be thought that there would be a significant relationship between the differences and changes in earnings described in Chapters 2 and 3 and the employment situation in the printing industry. The previous section has suggested that these differentials reflect the fact that the managements are unable to compete for labour and workers are restricted in their choice of job. Even so, Fleet Street is not entirely immune from competitive labour market pressures, since the trade unions cannot ignore the situation of their members in the printing industry. At the outset of the period, for example, there was a shortage of labour in the printing industry, and many witnesses before the Royal Commission on the Press, 1961-2, complained of the problems this caused.[20] By the end of the period the situation had changed dramatically. There was considerable unemployment due to the contraction of the printing industry in London and the Home Counties and there were also fears about the future of the *Sun* and the *Daily Sketch*.[21]

It is difficult to say what the findings in Chapters 2 and 3 might have been had this pattern been different and yet there is no evidence to suggest that it was of major significance. It is true that towards the end of the period there were marked changes in some of the controls described in the previous section in order to meet the challenge of the growing unemployment in the printing industry. The NGA, for example, terminated the apprenticeship agreement (for Stereotypers) and NATSOPA and SOGAT sought to limit the number of 'ghosts' and to end sixth-night working. Also, Chapters 8 and 10 will argue that the managements' ability to reduce *total* production wages was largely conditioned by the reaction of the trade unions to the employment situation. Yet the offices were affected equally by this employment situation and there is no evidence to suggest that any one occupation was affected more than the others. More significantly, there was no correlation between changes in earnings and the employment situation.[22] The period

20. See, for example, the Documentary and Oral Evidence of the BFMP to the Royal Commission on the Press, 1961-2.
21. In fact, the critical year was 1971. Some 600 members in the machine branch of NATSOPA and more than 1,000 members in the case of the LCB of SOGAT were reported to be looking for work.
22. Nor did occupational differentials widen as might be expected. Chapter 3 has already shown that these differentials fell steadily and substantially over the period.

1967 to 1970, for example, witnessed the largest increase in earnings and a slight improvement relative to manufacturing industry generally, yet this was the very period when the trade unions were beginning to feel the effects of the growing unemployment in the printing industry.

Decasualization

It might also be thought that there would be a significant relationship between the differences and changes in earnings and the decasualization which took place in the machine and publishing departments. An agreement between the NPA and LCB of SOGAT in 1963 led to the regularization of many casual members in the branch who were given a regular job on a Saturday night and three nights in the week. A similar agreement between the NPA and the machine branch of NATSOPA followed in 1966: this time the casual members who already worked four, three, and two fixed nights were given regular jobs. Other casual members were given regular jobs as the result of the negotiation of comprehensive agreements; Chapter 10 describes the agreements at the *Daily Mirror* and *Sunday Mirror* in some detail.

Again, it is difficult to say what the findings in Chapters 2 and 3 might otherwise have been, but there is no evidence to suggest that this decasualization was significant. The fact that the increases in earnings of occupations in the machine and publishing departments were below average is not explained by the costs of decasualization. 'Regular' casuals already received the same earnings and fringe benefits as regular workers and so the only major costs of decasualization were the indirect ones involved in regularizing 'casual' casuals. Neither must the extent of decasualization be exaggerated; Table 6.4 shows that many offices still made considerable use of casual working. To put the matter beyond reasonable doubt, Chapter 10 will show that the increase in costs as a result of decasualization was more than offset by the reduction, or below-average increase, in *total* production wages in the machine and publishing departments, following the negotiation of comprehensive agreements.

So the conclusions of this chapter too are negative. There is no evidence to suggest a significant relationship between the differences in earnings noted in Chapter 2 and the characteristics of the labour force in the different offices. It would also appear that the differences and changes in earnings noted in both Chapters 2 and 3 were settled by the managements and the chapels with little regard for supply and demand conditions in the labour market. This is because the managements are unable to compete for labour and workers cannot respond to differences and changes in the relative levels of pay by moving from office to office and from occupation to occupation. Furthermore, the employment situation in the printing industry and the decasualization in the machine and publishing departments do not seem to have had a direct influence.

Chapter 7

The Product Market

The demand for labour is derived from the demand for the product and so conditions in the product market might have influenced the findings in Chapters 2 and 3. With technology fixed in the short run, fluctuations in the demand for the product might have been a factor in the differences in earnings between offices noted in Chapter 2 and the changes in earnings noted in Chapter 3. Competition in the product market might also be significant. The competition between the newspapers takes many forms and differences between the newspapers might help to explain the differences in earnings.[1] Or the competition with other media might be significant. Finally, the ability of the different newspapers to absorb increases in production wages might also be a factor.

A Special Example of Joint Supply

Newspapers are a special example of joint supply and satisfy demands in two complementary product markets. Not only does the reader buy a copy of the newspaper for its news and information, but the advertiser also buys 'space' in the newspaper to display his goods and services. This section tests for relationships between the differences and changes in earnings noted in Chapters 2 and 3 and

1. The newspapers included in this study may be divided into the following categories: quality daily, popular daily, and evening newspapers. J. Curran has suggested that: 'The significant difference between the quality and popular newspaper is that while the quality publication aims at serving those who want full information on a wide range of public matters, and who are prepared to devote time to reading it, the popular publisher aims his product at those who want their news presented in a more summary way and with more illustration.' J. Curran, 'The Impact of TV on the Audience for National Newspapers, 1945-68' in J. Tunstall (ed.), *Media Sociology* (London: Constable, 1970).

the levels of activity in these two product markets.

Relationship between Earnings and Copy Sales[2]

Copy sales reflect readers' demand for newspapers but, for the purposes of this study, suffer from a number of deficiencies as a measure of the level of activity. The historical circumstances described later in this chapter have to be taken into account: the changes in copy sales during the 1960s may suggest conclusions which ignore the fact that some newspapers enjoyed artificially high levels in an earlier period. Moreover, the number of copies of the newspaper does not directly affect many of the occupations included in the study. Only the occupations in the machine and publishing departments and, to a lesser extent, in the maintenance departments are directly involved. The others are involved in the manufacture of the 'first copy' only.

Taking into account eight[3] of the offices, the statistical relationship between differences in the earnings of 'All Occupations' and differences in copy sales was very weak. The correlation coefficients were .2617 in 1961, .2637 in 1964, .0156 in 1967, and .3017 — in 1970. None of these coefficients is significant even at the 10% level; and the coefficient for 1970 is negative, reflecting the fact that by this date the earnings on the quality newspapers were higher in most cases than on the popular newspapers but the copy sales much less.

The relationship between changes in the earnings of 'All Occupations'[4] and changes in copy sales was stronger. The correlation coefficients were .3733 for the period 1961 to 1964, .8572 for the period 1964 to 1967, .1292 for the period 1967 to 1970, and .7356 for the period 1961 to 1970. The coefficients are significant at the 5% level for the periods 1964 to 1967 and 1961 to 1970, but are not significant for the other two periods.

2. Details of copy sales are from the Audit Bureau of Circulation reports for the period 1 July to 31 December in each year.
3. Two of the newspapers are not included throughout this section because of the lack of some essential data.
4. Increases in the industry basic rates have been ignored on the assumption that they multiply most of the components of pay, i.e. a percentage increase in the industry basic rates represents approximately the same percentage increase in earnings in each office. (See Chapter 4.)

Since it is largely determined by the amount of advertising, the average page size, or number of pages in the newspaper, is a measure of the level of activity in the market for advertisers. As such, it has the important advantage over copy sales that it directly affects most, if not all, of the occupations included in the study. The page size is also a useful guide to the economic situation of a newspaper, since an increase in page size suggests that the newspaper is securing, or hoping to secure, sufficient advertising revenue to cover the ever-increasing costs of newsprint. But the page size does have its deficiencies as a measure of the level of activity. If the number of pages 'published' is a fair reflection of the level of activity over time and in different offices, in some departments it may have little relationship to the number of pages actually produced. For example, there may be more editorial changes on issues with a smaller number of pages 'published'! More significantly, the average page size hides the very considerable fluctuations from day to day and from week to week. Only those newspapers which are the market leaders are able to dictate to the advertiser the day on which his advertisement will appear, and even they are loath to do so. An analysis of the daily page sizes of the daily newspaper for one year did not suggest that any one fluctuated more than others, but this was one year only.

The relationship between differences in the earnings of 'All Occupations' and differences in the page sizes was weak and negative in 1961, but positive and much stronger in the other three years studied. The correlation coefficients were .0716— in 1961, .6051 in 1964, .7758 in 1967, and .8422 in 1970. The coefficients are significant at the 10% level in 1964 and at the 5% level in 1967 and 1970.

The relationship between changes in the earnings of 'All Occupations' and changes in page size were stronger still. The correlation coefficients were .7529 for the period 1961 to 1964, .9618 for the period 1964 to 1967, .8536 for the period 1967 to 1970, and .8894 for the period 1961 to 1970. The coefficients are significant at the 5% level (and less) for each of the periods studied. The

5. Details of the page size in 1961 and 1964 were calculated for the calendar year from details of the number of pages in the EIU Report, assuming 310 issues each year. In 1967 and 1970 they are the average page size for the calendar year.

relationship between changes in earnings and changes in page size was also plotted on scatter diagrams and the results are shown in Diagrams 7.1 to 7.4. Diagram 7.3 is especially informative. It shows that not only did some of the newspapers suffer a reduction in earnings in the period 1964 to 1967 but also a reduction in page size.

Table 7.1 which ranks the offices in order depending on the changes in the earnings of 'All Occupations' and changes in page sizes, is also informative. In the period 1961 to 1964 office J, for example, had the lowest increase in earnings and in the period 1964 to 1967 the highest; in the period 1961 to 1964 it had the lowest increase in page size and in the period 1964 to 1967 the highest. Office H is also interesting. In the period 1961 to 1964 it had the second highest increase in earnings, in the period 1964 to 1967 the second lowest, and in the period 1967 to 1970 the highest; in the period 1961 to 1964 it had the third highest increase in page size, in the period 1964 to 1967 the second largest decrease, and in the period 1967 to 1970 the highest increase.

So it would appear that differences and changes in page sizes had some bearing on the findings in Chapters 2 and 3.[6] Differences in page size seem to help to explain the differences in earnings described in Chapter 2; and changes in page sizes seem to help to explain the changes in earnings described in Chapter 3.[7]

'Pure' Drift [8]

An investigation of the extent of 'pure' drift, i.e. the percentage

6. Yet a third measure of the level of activity is the total pagination of the newspapers, i.e. copy sales x average page size x the number of issues. The statistical relationship between differences and changes in the earnings of 'All Occupations' and differences and changes in total pagination was not as strong as that between changes in earnings and changes in page size.
7. With the exception of the period 1964 to 1967, when most of the correlation coefficients were positive and significant, it was difficult to find any common pattern in the relationship between changes in earnings of individual occupations and changes in page sizes.
8. E. H. Phelps Brown has defined 'pure' drift as 'changes in the effective rate of labour input . . . [caused] by arrangements that lie outside the recognized procedures of scheduling rates'. 'Wage Drift', *Economica* (Nov. 1962), p. 340. To distinguish 'pure' drift from the different varieties of drift described in Chapter 4, the latter are often referred to as 'statistical' drift. See, for example, the discussion in S. Lerner *et al.*, *Workshop Wage Determination* (Oxford: Pergamon, 1969), pp. 18f.

SCATTER DIAGRAMS: CHANGES IN EARNINGS, CHANGES IN PAGE SIZE: ALL OCCUPATIONS

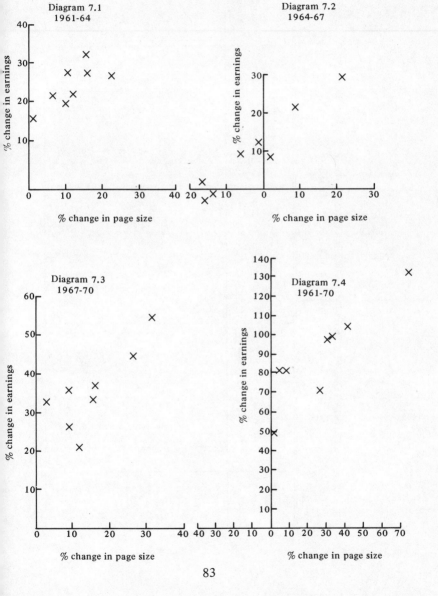

TABLE 7.1

RANKING OF OFFICES BY INCREASE IN AVERAGE WEEKLY EARNINGS AND PAGE SIZE: ALL OCCUPATIONS

Office	1961-1964		1964-1967		1967-1970		1961-1970	
	% Increase / Earnings	% Increase / Page Size	% Increase / Earnings	% Increase / Page Size	% Increase / Earnings	% Increase / Page Size	% Increase / Earnings	% Increase / Page Size
A	4	1	2	2	2	2	1	1
B	1	2=	5	3	4	7	4	4
C	7	5	8	7	7	6	8	8
D	6	7	4	5	6	8	5	7
F	3	6	6	8	3	3	6	6
H	2	2=	7	6	1	1	3	3
I	5	4	3	4	8	5	7	5
J	8	8	1	1	5	4	2	2

change in the earnings (per man) per unit of output less the percentage change in the industry basic rates,[9] confirms the importance of the relationship between changes in earnings and changes in page size. Tables 7.2 to 7.5, which give details of the average annual 'pure' drift in a number of the production departments, grouped under the headings 'Composing/Reading' and 'Foundry/Process', show that in most offices 'pure' drift was considerably less than the 'statistical'[10] drift noted in Chapter 4, as is to be expected if changes in earnings were associated with changes in page size. Significantly, in a number of offices 'pure' drift was negative; and in some there was a reduction in the earnings (per man) per unit of output, even taking into account increases in the industry basic rates.

Two further observations can be made. First, the fact that the

---

9. The following formula was used to calculate 'pure' drift:

$$PD = \frac{(EO_t - EO_{t-1})}{EO_{t-1}} - \frac{(W_t - W_{t-1})}{W_{t-1}} \quad 100$$

Where PD = pure drift
     EO = earnings (per man) per unit of output
     W = industry basic rate
     t = one year

Earnings (per man) per unit of output were calculated as follows: *Total* production wages for the period 1 July to 30 June were divided by the number employed. This figure in turn was divided by the number of pages produced, i.e. the average page size x the number of issues.

A word about the derivation of these variables may also be helpful. Details of *total* production wages are collected by the NPA each year for the purposes of calculating subscriptions. The number employed is the number employed in October each year and, for present purposes, includes day, night, and shift workers. For details of copy sales and page sizes, see notes 2 and 5 above. In each case these details have been adjusted to the year 1 July to 30 June. In the case of the newspapers which are also printed in Manchester, it is assumed that none of the pages used in London were produced in Manchester or, if they were, that they represented the same proportion from one year to the next. Unfortunately it was not possible to calculate earnings per unit of output for the machine and publishing departments. Casual working in these departments makes it difficult to say with any accuracy how many were employed. The number of regulars cannot be used on a time series basis because decasualization plays havoc with the figures. Furthermore, a measure of output in the machine and publishing departments must take into account total pagination, i.e. copy sales x average page size x the number of issues. The problem is that in the case of a number of the newspapers a not insignificant proportion of the number of copies produced comes from the Manchester office.

10. See note 8 above.

TABLE 7.2

AVERAGE ANNUAL PURE DRIFT: 1961-64

	A	B	C	D	E	F	G	H	I	J
Composing/Reading	0.7	2.4	2.8	−1.3	−3.7	4.9	−3.5	−1.1	−3.5	8.9
Foundry/Process	−2.2	1.1	−4.5	−4.0	−4.4	−2.6	−2.6	−1.2	−0.9	2.4

TABLE 7.3

AVERAGE ANNUAL PURE DRIFT: 1964-67

	A	B	C	D	E	F	G	H	I	J
Composing/Reading	−3.3	−1.0	3.6	3.1	—	6.2	—	4.2	0.4	−3.0
Foundry/Process	−9.0	2.5	1.2	−0.8	—	4.3	—	1.3	2.1	−1.4

TABLE 7.4

AVERAGE ANNUAL PURE DRIFT: 1967-70

	A	B	C	D	E	F	G	H	I	J
Composing/Reading	1.4	9.0	10.6	17.4	—	4.6	—	−0.4	4.3	2.3
Foundry/Process	−1.9	2.4	6.5	1.7	—	2.9	—	−13.9	3.4	−5.3

TABLE 7.5

AVERAGE ANNUAL PURE DRIFT: 1961-70

	A	B	C	D	E	F	G	H	I	J
Composing/Reading	−2.3	4.2	7.7	8.0	—	7.5	—	1.2	0.3	3.0
Foundry/Process	−5.2	2.6	1.1	−1.5	—	1.9	—	2.4	1.8	−1.8

offices with the largest increases in page size, office A, for example, were the offices with the lowest levels of 'pure' drift suggests that these offices enjoyed some of the advantages of the economies of scale. Secondly, in most of the offices 'pure' drift was greater in the period 1967 to 1970 and yet there was nothing exceptional about the increases in page size during this period. It would seem to follow, then, that the size of the payments negotiated by the managements and the chapels during this period was also greater.

Competition among the Newspapers

There is intense competition for readers and advertisers among the newspapers included in this study. As the Report of the Royal Commission on the Press, 1961-2, pointed out, 'internal competition between different types of publication and between publications of the same type is the dominant factor in the economics of most sections of the press.'[11] This section, then, examines the main forms of competition.

Table 7.6, which gives details of the retail prices of the daily and evening newspapers over the period 1961 to 1970, suggests no reason to believe that differences in retail prices will help to explain the differences described in Chapter 2. It is true that the quality newspapers, which charged higher prices, were also the higher paying offices, but then copy sales were much less. More significantly, Table 7.6 shows that within the categories of quality, popular, and evening newspapers not only were the retail prices the same or very similar but the changes were also uniform.

At first sight, the timing of the retail price changes suggests that they might have some bearing on the changes in earnings described in Chapter 3. In the period 1961 to 1967, with the exception of the *Financial Times*, there was only one retail price change per newspaper. In the period 1967 to 1970, which witnessed the highest increases in earnings, there were two. However, it is difficult to decide whether these retail price changes were cause or effect. For there is evidence whch suggests that these changes were themselves a *result* of the economic situation of the newspapers in which increases in production wages played a not insignificant part.[12]

11. *Report of the Royal Commission on the Press*, Cmnd. 1812 (London: HMSO, 1962), p. 57.
12. NBPI Reports Nos. 43 and 141, for example, both resulted from applications

TABLE 7.6
RETAIL PRICE CHANGES: DAILY AND EVENING NEWSPAPERS,
1961-70

Newspaper	Prices Charged in Old Pence									
	1961	1962	1963	1964	1965	1966	1967	1968	1969	1970
Quality dailies										
Daily Telegraph	3d				4d			5d		7.2d
The Times	5d		6d							12.0d
Guardian	4d			5d				6d		8.4d
Financial Times	4d	5d		6d			8d			12.0d
Popular dailies										
Daily Mirror	3d			4d				5d		6d
Daily Express	3d			4d				5d		6d
Daily Mail	3d					4d		5d		6d
Sun*	3d				4d			5d		6d
Daily Sketch	3d			4d				5d		6d
Evenings										
Evening News	3d			4d				5d		6d
Evng Standard	3d			4d				5d		6d

*Successor to the *Daily Herald* which ceased publication in September 1964
(Sources: NBPI and Labour Research Department)

Unlike the retail prices, there was no uniformity in the rates charged to the advertiser by the different newspapers.[13] Even newspapers within the same categories charged different rates, which were sometimes also the subject of discount arrangements. It is true that some of the quality newspapers which charged the higher rates were also higher paying, but here again copy sales were much less. Nor was there any correlation between changes in earnings and changes in advertising rates. Of the newspapers with above-average increases in advertising rates some had above- and some below-average increases in earnings. In short, there is no evidence to suggest that differences and changes in advertising rates had direct influence on the findings in Chapters 2, 3, and 4.

The other forms of competition are not so easy to assess. In the

---

under the 'Early Warning System' to increase prices in order to cover increases in costs. See NBPI Reports No. 43, *Costs and Revenue of National Daily Newspapers*, Cmnd. 5435 (London: HMSO, 1967) and No. 141, *Costs and Revenue of National Newspapers*, Cmnd. 4277 (London: HMSO, 1969).

13. The details have not been given here because, unlike the details of retail prices, they make it easier to decipher the code letters of some of the newspapers.

case of the editorial contents of the newspapers, for example, the *Report of the Royal Commission on the Press*, 1961-2, pointed out that 'it is hard to define what is a good newspaper and what is a bad newspaper, except in terms of the success which it has in attracting the readers whom it sets out to serve.'[14]

Late news and exclusive news are key ingredients in the editorial contents of the newspapers. Most publish a number of editions, in some cases running into double figures, which make it possible to update the news throughout the night or carry news that is exclusive to a particular region. A football match report is an excellent example. In some cases the newspapers are able to delay the northern editions hours longer by printing in Manchester.[15] Even so, the editions are not necessarily homogeneous products. There are usually a number of page changes within each edition; news reported in the 'stop press' of early copies is often transferred in a matter of minutes to the front page.

The significance of the page size of the newspapers has already been discussed in the previous section. The page size is also an important contributing factor to the editorial contents of a newspaper: the more pages, the more scope for news and features.

Competition in methods of distribution is ruled out (except between the two evening newspapers which have their own fleets of vans) because distribution arrangements are shared. The NPA negotiates collective contracts with British Rail for the carriage of newspapers. Terms are negotiated individually with representatives of the wholesalers and retailers but are usually the same within the categories.

A simple assessment of these different forms of competition is possible, however, if newspapers within the categories of quality, popular, and evenings are compared with one another. To all intents and purposes, these newspapers are direct substitutes for each other. As the *Report of the Royal Commission on the Press*, 1961-2, pointed out; 'in the popular national daily and Sunday press there is fierce competition for readers and advertisers; the quality Sunday newspapers engage in the same fierce competition, but it is not so harsh among the quality dailies.'[16]

14. *loc. cit.*
15. A list of the newspapers which print their northern editions in Manchester is contained in note 6 of Chapter 1.
16. *Report of the Royal Commission on the Press*, 1962, *loc. cit.*

When newspapers within the same category are compared with one another, there are some very remarkable results. The spread of earnings between the offices, which Chapter 2 found to be extremely large, reduces quite considerably, in some occupations the difference being nominal. In 1961 Permanent Time Hands on two quality newspapers, for example, were earning £24.15 and £24.62 per week; in 1964 Oilers on the two evening newspapers were earning £29.946 and £30.396; and in 1967 Oilers on two popular newspapers were earning £49.13 and £52.125. Thus it would appear that competition among newspapers within the same categories was also significant.

Competition with Other Media

It might also be thought that the competition with other media would be a factor. Provincial newspapers have always been in competition for readers and advertisers with the newspapers included in this study. They tend to have a monopoly of the local news and advertising; and this is especially true of the provincial daily and evening newspapers. Radio and television have also been competitors for many years. There are the late news programmes which anticipate much of the news appearing in the newspapers the following day. Then there are the regional programmes devoted to matters of local concern. Finally, and most importantly, there is the competition for advertisers from the Independent Broadcasting Authority companies.

However, there is no way of telling whether competition from the other media had direct bearing on the findings in Chapters 2, 3, and 4. The *Report of the Royal Commission on the Press*, 1961-2, put the problem succinctly when it said: 'The press as a whole has to compete with other suppliers of news and commentary as well as with other forms of leisure and on its performance in this form of competition depends its position among other advertising media.'[17]

Ability to Pay

It remains for this chapter to see if the ability to pay of the different

17. *ibid.*

newspapers was significant for the findings in Chapters 2, 3, and 4. Some newspapers might have had a smaller ratio of labour costs to total costs or been more price-elastic or more profitable, which would have made it easier for them to absorb increases in production wages.

There is little evidence to suggest that some newspapers would have found it easier to absorb increases in production wages because the ratio of labour costs to total costs was smaller. Table 7.7, which gives details of the costs of the daily newspapers as a percentage of total costs, suggests that the variation between offices was not very great. It is true that production wages were not the largest single item in total costs — a doubtful privilege enjoyed by newsprint. However, production wages were one of the largest single items over which the managements had some control, since the price of newsprint is determined in the world market.

Given the arguments of the two previous sections, there is also little evidence to suggest that some newspapers would have found it easier to absorb increases in production wages by increasing prices.[18] Witnesses before the Royal Commission on the Press, 1961-2, for example, argued that it would be madness for any newspaper other than the market leader to increase its retail price unilaterally.[19] Certainly, the uniformity of retail prices mentioned in a previous section suggests that few newspapers were prepared to challenge this view.

It is also important to remember that most of the newspapers whose economic situation appeared healthy because of increases in page sizes or copy sales were losing large sums of money each year. Table 7.8, for example, gives details of the results of eight daily newspapers in the period 1961 to 1966, showing that five were making losses.

The simple explanation for this situation is that the retail price of the newspaper does not produce sufficient revenue to cover the costs of production. Table 7.9, which gives details of how each 1d. from copy sales was spent in 1969, shows that the balance has to be made up, if at all, from advertising revenue, and this depends on the state of the economy as a whole. Newspapers, in short, have had little control over their own financial situation. Lord Devlin's comments

18. There is one possible exception to this statement. However, to name the newspaper in question might make it possible to decipher the code letters.
19. *Report of the Royal Commission on the Press*, 1962, *loc. cit.*, p. 60.

TABLE 7.7
COSTS OF NATIONAL DAILY NEWSPAPERS EXPRESSED AS PERCENTAGES OF TOTAL COSTS

	Quality		Popular		Total
	Group	Range within group	Group	Range within group	
	%	%	%	%	%
Newsprint and ink	28	19-34	33	23-29	31
Production costs	30	24-33	29	27-30	30
Sub-total	58	45-67	62	53-68	61
Circulation & distribution costs *	11	6-11	9	8-10	9
Sub-total	69	55-78	71	62-76	70
Editorial	15	12-23	17	13-24	16
Advertising	3	1-5	1	1-2	2
Publicity	4	2-6	2	1-5	3
Administration, establishment and management charges	9	7-14	9	9-12	9
Sub-total	31	22-45	29	24-38	30
Total	100	100	100	100	100
of which production wages account for	18	17-20	20	16-23	20

*Excluding distributors' discounts.
(Source: NBPI Report No. 141)

Note 1: The above figures are based on individual newspapers' results during their most recent accounting years and can be compared with Table 2 in Report No. 43.

Note 2: In the columns which show the ranges within each group, meaningful comparison of some individual cost items between newspapers is not possible because the companies employ different methods of allocating costs incurred jointly with other activities.

in his foreword to the EIU Report sum up the plight of the newspapers:

But ... there is one thing that strikes me personally on a first reading ... The forecast is that before this decade ends, if present trends continue, three more national dailies and one more national Sunday will have gone. They will not be swallowed up by tycoons anxious to foist their own brands of politics on increasing masses. There are no such people. This report destroys utterly the idea that newspapers can be forcibly kept alive by anti-monopoly legislation. If these newspapers die ... here is what their death certificate will say. A change in reading habits of the public caused a decline in the overall circulation — 10% in dailies and 23% in Sundays — and this chronic weakness was aggravated to fatality by an economic depression hitting the advertising revenue on which these newspapers, sold by the standards of other countries too cheaply, have become too dependent.

The low retail price of the newspapers is born of historical circumstances. Paper Control Orders issued by governments during World War II restricted the use of newsprint and the amount of space which would be devoted to advertising, thus preventing the newspapers from competing with one another in page size. Costs were therefore low and there was no need to increase price. But this was not all. Newspapers, which could only be secured on order, were unable to satisfy readers' demands. Multiple readership developed with members of the public buying more than one newspaper each. Copy sales soared, reaching a peak in 1951 and maintaining these levels, with some individual fluctuations, until 1957.

TABLE 7.8

NEWSPAPERS' RESULTS

	3 newspapers currently making profits £'000s	5 newspapers currently making losses £'000s	Net profits 8 newspapers £'000s
1961	4,930	(229)	4,701
1962	4,090	(495)	3,595
1963	5,465	(842)	4,623
1964	6,212	(4,074)	2,138
1965	9,511	(4,642)	4,869
1966	8,388	(4,329)	4,059

(Source: NBPI Report No. 43)

This sheltered market was shattered in 1956 when the controls on newsprint were finally removed.[20] The newspapers were unable

20. There was some attempt to continue the controls on a voluntary basis until 1959.

93

TABLE 7.9
REVENUE AND COSTS OF NATIONAL NEWSPAPERS EXPRESSED IN PENCE PER COPY SOLD[a]

	Dailies		Sundays	
	Quality	Popular	Quality	Popular
Number of newspapers	3	5	3	4
Revenue and cost per copy	d	d	d	d
Sales revenue[b]	3.40	3.27	7.06	4.66
Advertising revenue	8.53	1.69	23.81	3.21
Other revenue	0.09	0.04	0.21	0.04
Total Revenue	12.02	5.01	31.08	7.91
Newsprint and ink	3.54	1.51	7.82	2.35
Circulation and distribution	1.32	0.38	4.81	0.78
Total newsprint and distribution	4.86	1.89	12.63	3.13
Production costs	3.74	1.35	9.35	2.10
Editorial costs	1.98	0.77	4.26	0.89
Administrative costs	1.14	0.45	1.93	0.62
Other fixed costs	0.81	0.15	2.53	0.25
Total editorial and overheads	3.93	1.37	8.72	1.76
Total costs[c]	12.53	4.61	30.70	6.99
Profit	(0.51)	0.40	0.38	0.92
Size of paper[d]	Pages	Pages	Pages	Pages
Advertising	11.4	4.3	28.5	10.1
Editorial	15.6	8.3	25.2	11.5
Total	27.0	12.6	53.7	21.6
Percentage of space devoted to advertising	% 42	% 34	% 53	% 46

(Source: NBPI Report No. 141)

a   The figures are based on individual newspapers' results during their most recent accounting years and can be compared with Table 3 in Report No. 43.

b   Not of discounts to distributors.

c   Meaningful comparison of some individual cost items between newspapers is not possible because the companies employ different methods of allocating costs incurred jointly with other activities.

d   For this table all newspapers have been converted to a standard page size of 17½ inches by 22½ inches.

to resist exploiting their monopoly of advertising, and began to compete with one another. Page sizes inevitably increased, taking with them newsprint costs, which were already increasing in their own right. Copy sales began to decline from their peak. The newspapers were larger and so there was a decline in multiple readership; television too was beginning to take its toll. Furthermore, any attempt to increase retail price in order to cover costs only exaggerated the decline in copy sales. The public had become used to a low price; and any increase represented a large percentage increase, especially when reflected in the newsagent's bill at the end of each week or month. This, then, is the background which helps to explain the economic situation of the newspapers during the period with which this study is concerned.

But some of the newspapers were making profits and it remains to be seen if their ability to pay is reflected in the differences and changes in earnings described in Chapters 2 and 3. The data, like all data relating to the profitability of holding companies, are difficult to interpret, and if presented here would reveal the identity of the newspapers concerned. It is possible, however, to make one or two significant observations. Some of the newspapers making profits were among the higher paying offices and those with above-average increases in earnings. But in each case there was also an increase in page size and copy sales. One newspaper making profits was not among the higher paying offices or those with above-average increases in earnings. In this particular case page sizes and copy sales were relatively stable. Finally, some of the newspapers which were among the higher paying offices and had above-average increases in earnings were making losses, but in these cases there were also increases in page sizes and copy sales. In other words, profitability alone does not appear to have been significant.

To summarize, then, this chapter has established that there was a positive and significant relationship between the differences and changes in earnings and differences and changes in page sizes. It has also suggested that the competition between the newspapers was significant: workers employed on newspapers which to all intents and purposes are direct substitutes for each other had very similar earnings. Otherwise, the conclusions have been negative. In particular, it has been suggested that profitability alone does not appear to be significant. But for a fuller understanding of the findings of this and the two previous chapters the study must now examine the attitudes and policies of the parties. The chapels are the first to be considered.

Chapter 8

The Chapels

The chapel is the name used to describe the workshop organizations of workers in the printing and newspaper industries. It was first used to describe the organizations of compositors and pressmen, and the earliest reference is to be found in a work published in 1683.[1] By the turn of the eighteenth century these chapels had become trade union organizations which later were to link up to form trade unions proper.[2] As other groups of workers in the printing and newspaper industries have organized themselves, so clerical workers, journalists and maintenance workers have adopted the chapel as the form of workshop organization.

The rule books of the trade unions provide few clues about the membership of chapels beyond stating that the members employed in an establishment must form themselves into a chapel. The rules of the NGA, for example, state that: 'In every office recognised by the Association there shall be at least one chapel and an appointed Father of the Chapel.' In Fleet Street, however, it is possible to identify a consistent pattern. With the exception of the members of the RIRMA branch of NATSOPA, who are spread over a number of occupations and departments, there is a chapel for each group of union members in a department; in some cases there are also separate chapels for day and night workers. Only the overseers, who have to be members of the union, are exempt. Tables 8.1 and 8.2

---

1. J. Moxon writes, 'Every Printing-house is by custom of time out of mind called a Chappel; and all the workmen who belong to it are members of the Chappel; and the oldest Freeman is Father of the Chappel.' *Mechanick Exercises*, 1683 (1896 edition), p. 356.
2. See, for example, A. J. M. Sykes, 'Trade Union Workshop Organisation in the Printing Industry — the Chapel', *Human Relations* (Feb. 1960). See also E. Howe and H. E. Waite, *The London Society of Compositors* (London: Cassell, 1948), and A. E. Musson, *The Typographical Association* (London: Oxford University Press, 1954).

TABLE 8.1

TRADE UNIONS: RELATIONSHIP OF MEMBERS TO FULL-TIME OFFICIALS

Union	Members		Chapels		Full-time Branch Officials	Members per Full-time Branch Official	Chapels per Branch Officials	Average Members per Chapel		
	Branch Total	in NPA Offices	Branch Total	in NPA Offices				Branch	in NPA Offices	in non-NPA Offices
NUJ	3,100	1,700	60	17	1	3,100	60	51	100	32
NGA	23,850	4,450	1,135	59	8a	2,980	142	21	75	18
SLADE	6,500	450	300	14	3a	2,250	100	21	32	20
NATSOPA										
Machine Branch	8,600	5,500	320	36	2	4,300	160	20	150	10
Clerical	11,000	4,591	108	15	2	5,500	54	102	306	71
RIRMA	6,375	2,500	220	70	1	6,375	220	28	35	26
SOGAT	30,000	b	1,150	21	5a	6,000	230	26	b	b

(Source: EIU Report)

a Excluding Financial Secretary

b Not available

TABLE 8.2

SIZE OF CHAPELS IN FLEET STREET

Unions	Total Number of Chapels	Distribution of Chapels by Size (Eleven newspaper offices included)						
		—10	11-25	20-50	51-100	101-200	201-500	500+
NATSOPA and SOGAT	128	17	26	23	21	13	19	9
NGA	51	4	11	20	12	3	1	—
SLADE	11	1	2	8	—	—	—	—
NUJ	10	—	—	—	1	8	1	—
AUEW	12	2	3	5	2	—	—	—
EETU	10	1	—	4	5	—	—	—

(Source NPA, 1970)

give the results of recent inquiries into the number and size of the chapels in Fleet Street.

In accordance with the rules of the trade unions, each chapel is required to elect a Father of the Chapel, known usually as the FOC. In most of the unions the period of office is one year but in NATSOPA it is three months. In Fleet Street the chapels are likely to have a number of officials. In the larger chapels there is the FOC, a deputy FOC, one or more clerks or secretaries, and a chapel or management committee with a chairman and some half dozen members. FOCs in the machine and publishing departments are usually non-working, and other members of the committee are likely to have jobs which allow them to spend most, if not all, their time on chapel business. In the smaller chapels the FOC usually has to work, fitting in chapel business when necessary. In both large and small chapels the officials are paid the earnings of their occupation; they may also receive an honorarium and delegation fees from the chapel, together with expenses. FOCs in the larger chapels usually have their own office provided by the management. Most chapels have access to some office facilities; many have their own headed note paper.

Meetings of the chapel usually take place quarterly, and it is obligatory for members to attend on pain of a fine. These meetings are extremely formal. Motions must be in the hands of the clerk or secretary well in advance and the agenda is circulated two or three days before the meeting. The meetings begin with the reading of the minutes of the previous meeting; this is followed by the financial statement and the FOC's report. Questions are tabled and motions discussed. The chapel or management committee usually meets weekly, calling emergency meetings of the chapel when necessary.

The financial aspects of the chapels' administration are no less sophisticated. As well as paying the normal dues to the trade union, members also subscribe to a number of independent funds organized by the chapel which usually include those providing for sickness and retirement. In the larger chapels the clerk's or secretary's job may be divided into two, one having special responsibility, with the trustees, for the chapel's finances.

In most of the newspaper offices in Fleet Street there is also a Federated House Chapel to which all the chapels belong. This, however, has very little authority and only negotiates with the management on such matters as company pensions and car parking arrangements. One recent development in Fleet Street has been the organization of members of the NGA into an Imperial Chapel with an Imperial FOC. Individual chapels still retain their autonomy, however, and in many offices Stereotypers and Machine Managers are not members.

There is one important point to be made before examining the goals and constraints of the chapels. The same care has to be taken as in the later chapter on the managements. A chapel in Fleet Street may have hundreds of members. It is not suggested that they all think the same about an issue. Indeed, there may be interest groups within the chapel and chapel officers may have personal motives for the policies they support. While, therefore, this study follows common usage in using the chapel to describe the collectivity of its members, it is important to bear these qualifications in mind. The same qualifications are necessary when considering general statements made in this chapter about the various chapels in the offices. Because of the differences between them general statements are only made to illustrate predominant features about Fleet Street.

Goals and Constraints

The constraints imposed by the managements in Fleet Street on the goals of the chapels as trade union organizations are no different in kind from those imposed by managements in other industries. There is the competition for scarce economic resources; production wages are a significant proportion of total costs which the managements are anxious to minimize. But authority and power are also scarce. The decisions which the managements take to satisfy their goals and constraints in the product market are often at odds with the interests of workers as the latter see them. However, the constraints imposed by the managements in Fleet Street are different in degree because of the special characteristics of the product market.

It might be thought, for example, that the threat of closures which seems to have hung over Fleet Street for so many years would have had a profound effect on the attitudes and policies of the chapels. But with rare exceptions,[3] this has not been the case; there is little

3. The trade unions did agree to make certain sacrifices in terms of payments and practices in order to keep the *Guardian* and *Sun* going in 1966. The fact that this does not happen more often might seem surprising. But, as Chapter 10 will show, there are less obvious ways in which the newspapers are able to adjust to a decline in their economic position.

evidence to suggest that the economic situation has been experienced as a constraint. There is undoubtedly a credibility gap; despite the warnings of closure, the money somehow seems to be found and the newspaper continues to be published. Indeed, the fact that in many cases the future of the newspaper is entirely dependent on the whim of the proprietor unrelated to any discernible measure of economic performance is not without significance. It can be argued that recognition of this has bred attitudes of irresponsibility with little thought for the longer term.

It is the discontinuities in production which pose the biggest day-to-day threat to the interests of members of the chapels. Each issue of the newspaper, it must be remembered, is a different product; the page size, lay-out, the type and quantity of advertising — all these are likely to be different. But even each issue is not a homogeneous product. Editions too are virtually different products. Then there are the page changes: a recent inquiry in one office established that the setting charges in the composing department were higher on a 24pp. than a 48pp. issue because the editorial department used the extra time to make additional changes. Late news and exclusive news too present problems in terms of peaks in activity and special manning requirements. All these discontinuities disrupt working arrangements. Before the negotiation of comprehensive agreements, they threatened the stability of earnings as well. Last, but not least, in the machine and publishing departments these discontinuities threaten employment itself, since many workers are employed on a casual basis only.

This type of situation makes it essential for the chapels to seek some control over the impact of changes in the product and fluctuations in the level of activity in the product market. But it also gives them the ability to do this simply and effectively: all they have to do is to insist that the managements negotiate with their representatives whenever these changes and fluctuations result in a need to alter working arrangements.[4]

Of course, today the chapels do not necessarily explain their behaviour in this way. There is an important learning process

4. In these respects the situation in Fleet Street is not dissimilar to that described by J. Kuhn in his study of 'fractional bargaining': 'First, it subjects a large proportion of the workers to continued changes in work methods, standards or materials as they work at individually paced jobs. Second, it allows workers a considerable degree of interaction in their task group as they work at their

involved. For reasons which will become clearer in Chapter 10, the chapels have been able to achieve a remarkable degree of control over the immediate work situation. The first-line managers, or overseers as they are known in Fleet Street, have little executive responsibility in most departments. It is often the FOC who recruits the labour and allocates it to the different tasks. It is the FOC who draws up the overtime and holiday rotas. It is also the FOC and chapel committee who are responsible for discipline. In effect, then, it is the FOC who is the man-manager. But this control has now become second nature. For example, it has been recognized that '. . . workers who are allowed to make decisions at their work come to feel more possessive of that work, workers who are left alone and so have come to take their work for granted will also, when threatened, resent such interference.'[5] The EIU Report too remarked that:

Newspaper workers often fail to realise that their industry is almost unique in the degree to which control of labour is in the hands of the Unions. The fact that quite large numbers of men spend a large proportion of their working lives negotiating, taking part in deputations and meetings among themselves is not thought to be at all unusual.[6]

It must be emphasized that this does not apply only in those departments with a craft technology. It is equally true of members of NATSOPA and SOGAT

The learning process is also important in another respect. It may seem strange that individual members of the chapels have only exchanged the controls imposed by the managements for those imposed by the chapel and the trade union. But these too have become second nature. The chapel is seen to be the body that makes the important decisions about working arrangements. Its authority is legitimate in the eyes of the members. Moreover, if there is a

---

distinctive and specialised semi-skilled jobs. Third, it groups most of the work into several nearly equal sized task departments. Fourth, it requires continuous rigidly sequential processing of materials into one major type of product.' The first and second characteristics, Kuhn suggests, 'stimulate the willingness of the members of the work group to engage in fractional bargaining'. The third 'tends to weaken the political authority of the local union over the work group'. The fourth 'enables the work group to disrupt the plant's production at a cost which is small in relation to the cost it inflicts on management'. *Bargaining in Grievance Settlement* (New York: Columbia University Press, 1961), p. 148.

5. R. Holmes, 'The Ownership of Work: A Psychological Approach', *British Journal of Industrial Relations* (March 1967), p. 25.

6. p. 93.

'dictatorship' of the chapel, at least the officers can be voted out and policies changed.[7]

The fact that the great majority of workers in the occupations included in this study have already worked in the printing industry is also significant. They have been members of other chapels and so have come to experience the customs and traditions of the chapel. To quote Sykes:

Despite the size and geographical dispersion of the industry, chapels throughout the country display a remarkable uniformity. A printer moving from one works to another finds himself a member of a chapel fundamentally similar to the one he has left. A new works staffed by printers from various places will produce chapels of the standard pattern. There may be slight variations in detail but throughout the country printers' chapels conform to one basic pattern.[8]

It is important to remember too that the chapel is more than a trade union organization. Sykes, for example, has suggested that the chapel is 'not one group with a single purpose but is . . . a multi-purpose group — an amalgamation of several different kinds of groups each with its own purpose and functions'.[9] First, he suggests, there was the informal group, 'arising out of the social relations between people in face to face contact'. Secondly, there was the common interest group: 'these associations were not set up for any one single purpose, such as negotiation with the employer, but associations to govern and regulate all matters concerning the group'. Thirdly, there was the traditional group: 'each new chapel inherited a body of custom which determined its functions and constitution and brought it into line with other chapels'. Fourthly, there was the trade organization: 'when chapels came together to form local trade unions which later amalgamated as national printing unions . . . the chapels took on the additional duty of being the trade union organisation within the workshop'. Sykes's conclusion is that 'the trade union organisation gains its strength from the fact that it is grafted onto an existing and highly developed form of workshop organisation'.[10]

7. The phrase 'democratic dictatorship' was actually used by one ex-FOC in a conversation with the author. In fact, the chapels are an excellent example of the theoretical model of work group behaviour outlined by Fox. See A. Fox, *A Sociology of Work in Industry* (London: Collier-Macmillan, 1971).
8. A. J. M. Sykes, 'The Cohesion of a Trade Union Workshop Organisation', *Sociology* (May 1967), p. 146.
9. *ibid.*, p. 155.
10. *ibid.*, p. 156. The desire to protect a highly prized skill is the most probable

There are also a number of rules and regulations enforced by the chapels to ensure that the interests of the individual members do not conflict with those of the chapel as a whole. The chapel negotiates standard rates or payments for all its members, individual payments being excluded except in the case of payments for service. Individual members are discouraged from communicating with the managements. Individual grievances are chapel grievances; and communications from the managements have to be channelled through chapel officers.[11] Should conflicts of interest between the individual member and the chapel occur, the chapels have a number of sanctions at their disposal to bring the recalcitrant member into line. Besides the informal sanctions available to any work group, there are fines, imposed by the chapel or the trade union, and the ultimate sanction of expulsion which, in the printing industry, is tantamount to dismissal from employment.

A second set of constraints is imposed on the chapels by the trade unions. The control of the unions by the membership is, in the words of the NGA rule book, 'based on the chapel' but the chapels are still subject to the rules and instructions of the parent bodies which have more authority than in most other industries because of their control of labour supply. Failure to comply with union rules and instructions may incur fines and, in the last resort, expulsion. Most of the printing unions also issue guidance to the chapels on the drafting of rules. In most cases this takes the form of a framework containing such basic essentials as the frequency of elections and the method of

---

explanation for the development of the chapel in the printing industry, plus the fact that the literacy which accompanied the skill was unique. In seeking to account for the cohesion of the chapel, Sykes places great store by custom because it lays down guiding principles and practices. He argues that there are three major factors necessary to the endurance of custom, all of which are present in the printing industry. First, there is time itself: the chapel has been established as an institution for over three hundred years. Secondly, there must be continuity and the means of transmitting custom from one generation to another. In the printing industry continuity has been ensured by the slow rate of technological change and the stability of the labour force. The apprenticeship system has provided a means of training entrants in the social as well as the technical traditions of the industry. Thirdly, the observance of custom also depends on the recognition by individuals of mutual obligations, and in the printing industry this is facilitated by the existence of relatively small work groups.

11. In 1972, in fact, the managements found themselves in some difficulty in their efforts to comply with the requirement of the Industrial Relations Act that each individual employee should receive notice of changes in his contract of employment!

voting. The framework is then added to by the chapels themselves and the final set of rules passed to the branch committee for their approval.[12]

The sanctions exist and yet are rarely used. In most cases there is no conflict. Sykes, for example, has pointed out that the chapels perform two trade union functions: the chapel 'carries out the duties laid upon it by the trade union in enforcing trade union rules and agreements and carrying out trade union functions in the workshop';[13] it also makes and enforces 'collective decisions on all matters within the works which are of interest to them'.[14] But the chapels in Fleet Street enjoy a considerable degree of autonomy in spite of the formal position set out in the trade union rules.[15] There are several reasons for this. The chapels in Fleet Street are among the largest in the printing unions, in some cases totalling six or seven hundred members. They are extremely influential in trade union elections and many of the full-time officers are elected on the Fleet Street vote. Then there is the weakness of the managements. Many of the full-time officers are reluctant to oppose the policies of a chapel with which they disagree because they fear that the management will inevitably back down, and so undermine their authority. A recent example will illustrate the point. A full-time officer became involved in negotiations over a comprehensive agreement. Annoyed by what he believed to be delaying tactics on the part of the chapel and thinking the management's offer to be fair, he instructed the chapel to conclude the agreement. The FOC resigned, saying that he personally would not disobey the instruction but he feared that the chapel would. Subtle pressure by the chapel led the management to increase its offer over and above what the officer had instructed the chapel to accept. It needs very little imagination to guess what the reaction of the officer was!

12. The rules of the NGA, for example, state that: 'When four or more members are employed in an organised office, they shall be required to draw up rules for chapel administration purposes. Chapel rules shall be submitted to the respective branch committees for approval before becoming operative. Failure to carry out these obligations shall render the members of a chapel liable to suspension from benefit.'
13. A. J. M. Sykes, 'Trade Union Organisation in the Printing Industry — the Chapel', *op. cit.*, p. 55.
14. *ibid.*, p. 57.
15. Full-time officers made light of the chapels' autonomy to the Royal Commission on the Press, 1961-2. See, for example, the Written Evidence of the LTS and NATSOPA.

A third set of constraints is imposed by other chapels in the office. At first sight, this may seem surprising and yet in Fleet Street it is difficult to escape from the conclusion that other chapels exercise the most significant constraint. These other chapels are competitors for scarce economic resources and status. There is little or no co-operation between chapels in the same office. The Federated House Chapel has limited authority and rarely negotiates with the management; even the NGA Imperial Chapel does not include Stereotypers and Machine Managers in many offices. Traditional differentials inevitably shape the expectations of the chapels in negotiations; the dispute described in Appendix I is an excellent example of what is likely to happen if a management disappoints these expectations. The result is that the managements, like the NPA in its relationships with trade unions, have very little room in which to manoeuvre. Lines of demarcation are also jealously guarded. Fleet Street was the scene of a number of costly demarcation disputes in the period.

The explanation for the separatism of the chapels is partly historical: the division of labour into different crafts each with its craft society which was able to control the supply of labour did much to lay the foundation of the autonomy of individual chapels. The emergence of NATSOPA and SOGAT which had to face the problems of casual working added further interest groups. The fact of organization is also significant in its own right: each chapel has a hierarchy of leadership and formalized procedures which tend to be self-perpetuating. Moreover, the chapels have the power to make autonomy work. All these reasons, then, help to explain why they have not felt the need to develop coalitions, as workers in other industries have done.

Attitudes and Policies towards Pay

The chapels determine the timing and the size of pay claims and it would also seem that they have the power to impose their demands. This explains why it is necessary to establish whether or not their attitudes and policies help to explain the findings in Chapters 2, 3 and 4.

Despite what has been said above, this section begins by looking for evidence of policies of solidarity or 'the common rule'.[16] In Fleet Street, however, a number of possibilities have to be considered.[17] Such policies could take the form of attempts to achieve equality of earnings on the part of chapels whose members are in the same occupation but in different offices. Or it could take the form of attempts to achieve some felt-fair relationship between earnings on the part of chapels whose members are in the same union in the same office but in different occupations. Finally, it could take the form of attempts to improve the relative earnings of lower-paid workers irrespective of union.

On the face of it, there is little evidence to support the first possibility. Chapter 2 found that for some occupations the difference between the highest and lowest paying offices was more than 100%. In most cases there was no reduction in the dispersion of earnings, and in some there was an increase. Only the Engineers and Electricians show a significant reduction in the period 1967 to 1970. This might be cited as an example of the findings in Chapter 2 conforming to a policy of solidarity since it was the explicit policy of the two branches in question to seek to reduce the gap between the highest and lowest paying offices.

There is some evidence to support the second possibility. The narrowing in differentials between the Permanent Time Hands and Readers, on the one hand, and the Linotype Operators and Piece Case Hands, on the other, is consistent with the policy of the NGA and its predecessor, the LTS. In some offices this was facilitated by the formation of an Imperial NGA chapel which began to negotiate

16. It was Sidney and Beatrice Webb who wrote that 'among trade union regulations there is one which stands out as practically universal, namely, the insistence on payment according to some definite standard, uniform in its application.' *Industrial Democracy* (London: Longmans, Green, 1897), p. 279.
17. H. M. Douty has argued that: 'The application of the concept of the 'standard rate' to the wage structure of a modern factory is much more complicated than its application in industries . . . where the division of labour is along relatively clear-cut craft lines . . . Under these circumstances, the trade union approach to the 'standard rate' must take the general form of attempting to secure (1) equal pay for jobs of equal skill or difficulty; (2) a system of wage rate differentials that in some sense reflect the relative worth of the jobs, or groupings of jobs, within the enterprise.' 'The Impact of Trade Unionism on Internal Wage Structures', in J. L. Meij (ed.), *Internal Wage-Structure* (Amsterdam: North Holland, 1963), pp. 225-6.

on behalf of all NGA members in the composing and reading departments.

The situations in the electrical and engineering departments also offer an interesting contrast. The fact that the differentials between Electricians and Electricians' Assistants were less than those between Engineers and Engineers' Assistants is not without significance. Electricians' Assistants are members of the EETPU and there is a single chapel representing both occupations. Engineers' Assistants, on the other hand, are members of NATSOPA and not the AUEW. Unlike the Electricians' Assistants, there are no possibilities of promotion to journeyman status. Indeed, the two occupations have separate chapels. NATSOPA chapels in the machine department provide yet another example of attempts to equalize the earnings of members of the same union. In a number of offices the relative position of members in the lower grades in the machine department has been improved by promoting them to a higher grade. The result is that in some offices General Assistants, for example, earn the same as Magazine Hands or Oilers.

But there is no evidence to support the possibility that the general narrowing in differentials noted in Chapter 3 was due to attempts to improve the relative earnings of lower-paid workers regardless of union. As the previous section has already pointed out, the machinery for doing this was lacking, and there was no evidence of attention.

Maximization of Earnings

It might be thought that the chapels, which enjoy many, if not all, of the advantages of the monopolist,[18] would seek to maximize their members' earnings independently of what other chapels did. At first

18. The best-known work which develops the model of the trade union seeking to achieve some quantifiable objective is that of Dunlop. He argues that: 'An economic theory of a trade union requires that the organisation be assumed to maximise (or minimise) something.' J. T. Dunlop, *Wage Determination under Trade Unions* (New York: Macmillan, 1944), p. 3. He suggests a number of possible 'maximands' which, in essence, may be reduced to three: the wages per member, the employment of members; and the total wage bill. Of course this model is not without its critics, as later notes will show. For a straightforward analogy between a typical craft trade union and a monopolistic producer, see L. C. Hunter and D. J. Robertson, *Economics of Wages and Labour* (London: Macmillan, 1969), pp. 273-4.

sight, many of the findings in Chapters 2, 3 and 4 do seem to conform to such a policy. Earnings in Fleet Street are considerably higher than in manufacturing industry generally; they are also higher than in most other sections of the printing industry. There are the large number and variety of the components of pay described in Chapter 4 which might be explained by assuming that the chapels take every opportunity to increase their members' earnings. (The practice of negotiating many of the house extras in the form of overtime payments has the added advantage that the latter increase pro rata with increases in the industry basic rates.) Their reluctance to discontinue the practice of negotiating increases in the industry basic rates might be explained in the same way; it is simply another method of increasing their members' earnings.

A number of the findings in other chapters also seem to conform to a policy of maximizing earnings. There is the association between differences and changes in earnings and page sizes observed in Chapter 7 which can be explained by assuming that the chapels insist that their members should be compensated for increase in workload, and that they should share in any increase in revenue. There is the sixth night working described in Chapter 6: regulars work an additional shift often at the expense of casuals or the unemployed. Then there is the practice of 'ghost' or 'shortage' payments also described in Chapter 6. By working 'short' of the agreed staffing level the chapels are able to increase their members' earnings still further, the earnings of the 'ghost' men being shared by those present.

The willingness of many chapels to negotiate comprehensive agreements involving a reduction in the number of jobs also conforms to a policy of maximizing earnings. Anxious to find ways and means of increasing their members' earnings in spite of the constraints of the Labour government's incomes policy, they 'sold' jobs with little regard, critics within the unions argued, for 'casual' casuals who had no fixed pattern of working, or for those members in the printing industry who wished to get jobs in Fleet Street.[19] The example of IPC Newspapers which will be quoted in Chapter 10 gives some idea of the number of jobs reduced in one office; similar numbers were reduced in other offices.

And yet if many of the findings do seem to conform to a policy of

19. See, for example, the criticisms in T. Cliff, *The Employers' Offensive — Productivity Agreements and How To Fight Them* (London: Pluto Press, 1969).

income maximization, there are many that still remain unanswered.[20] Earnings in Fleet Street may be considerably higher than in manufacturing industry and other sections of the printing industry, but why are they not higher? Why were there such large differences among the offices? Why were increases in some occupations greater than in others? Why were there differences among the three periods? Then there is the lack of association between earnings and ability to pay found in Chapter 7. How is this explained by a policy of maximizing earnings?

There are other reasons for doubting the bearing of a policy of maximizing earnings on the findings in Chapters 2 and 3. Chapter 10 will show that there were reductions in *total* production wages in a number of offices. Also, it will show that the offices which were able to achieve a reduction in *total* production wages (or an increase smaller than the increase in earnings) were not the offices with above-average increases in earnings. More significantly, it appears that the departments in which these reductions took place, 'Foundry/Process', 'Machine', and 'Publishing', were not the departments with the above-average increases in earnings. Put another way, if the chapels in these departments did seek to maximize their members' earnings by agreeing to reduce the number of jobs, then they were not nearly as successful as the chapels in the composing and reading departments which did not.

20. The model of the trade union as a monopoly has been criticized on two accounts. Ross, for example, has argued that: 'As a matter of fact, many of the most interesting questions concerning union behaviour cannot be answered by any strictly economic analysis — why the most compelling wage comparisons often have so little to do with labour market conditions, why unions strike over small differences, why some wage differentials are ignored although others are attacked, why it is important to unions that they achieve higher real wages through higher money wages and so on.' A. M. Ross, *Trade Unions Wage Policy* (Berkeley: University of California Press, 1948), p. 4. Ross and others have also attacked the assumptions of this model. Wootton, for example, argues that: '. . . any attempt to explain trade union activity in terms of models based on monopolistic selling involves an important fallacy. For a trade union is not a monopolistic seller of labour: it is not a seller of labour at all, but a representative of individual sellers — which is something quite different.' B. Wootton, *The Social Foundations of Wage Policy* (London: Allen and Unwin, 1955), p. 72. Flanders, too, rejects the view that collective bargaining is 'a collective equivalent and alternative to individual bargaining', arguing that it is essentially a rule-making process. A. Flanders, 'Collective Bargaining: A Theoretical Analysis', in *Management and Trade Unions* (London: Faber and Faber, 1970). pp. 213ff.

There are a number of reasons for thinking that the chapels might have sought to maximize the number of jobs in their department. The members tend to look upon the trade unions as the source of employment because of their control over the supply of labour. There is the competition among the members in the printing industry to secure jobs in Fleet Street because of the high earnings. Family relationships also play a part: the members in Fleet Street have friends and relatives in the printing industry who are anxiously waiting for an opportunity to join them. Then there is the special problem of casual working in the machine and publishing departments. NATSOPA and SOGAT had been forced to organize all the workers in the casual pool in order to protect them against the threat of alternative supplies of labour. Once they had organized the pool, they were obligated to find the members work, preferably with the security of a regular job — hence the desire to decasualize as many jobs as possible. Finally, these pressures to maintain and, if possible, increase the number of jobs were intensified by unemployment in the printing industry towards the end of the period.

A number of findings in this study do seem to conform to a policy of employment maximization. Some chapels refused under any circumstances to negotiate comprehensive agreements involving a reduction in the number of jobs. Most refused to negotiate comprehensive agreements involving such reductions in the latter part of the period because of the unemployment in the printing industry. Over-manning is still to be found in most departments: the NBPI recognized that there had been some changes but concluded that the scope for further improvements was 'still considerable'.[21] The 'blow system' in the machine and publishing departments is yet another example of a practice which helps to increase the number of jobs. In one office, for example, the EIU Report maintained that in the publishing department there were 'more men on "blow" than working at any one time'![22] Then there is the decasualization in the

21. NBPI Report No. 141, *Costs and Revenue of National Newspapers*, Cmnd. 4277 (London: HMSO, 1969), p. 13.
22. p. 203. The term 'blow' is used, in the words of the EIU Report, to describe 'time away from the work-place for rest purposes'. It is a practice organized by the chapel which seems to have begun with continuous running in the machine department. In one office, for example, it appears that workers enjoyed two meal

112

machine and publishing departments. Agreements between the NPA and the two branches involved provided for the regularization of a considerable number of jobs in both departments; many comprehensive agreements, like those which will be described in Chapter 10, also provided for an increase in the number of regular jobs.

The list of characteristics which are consistent with a policy of maximizing employment is impressive, and yet it would be wrong to exaggerate the significance of such a policy. Chapter 10 will show that there were reductions in the number of jobs in many offices due to the negotiation of comprehensive agreements. Furthermore, the offices with above-average increases in *total* production wages, indicating an increase in the number of jobs, were also the offices with above-average increases in earnings. Then there is the situation in the machine and publishing departments. The fact that increases in earnings in these departments were below average is not explained by increases in the number of jobs. Chapter 10 will also show that there were reductions in *total* production wages in these departments which more than offset the increases as a result of decasualization.

But this leaves the paradox in behaviour in negotiating comprehensive agreements to be explained. It can be explained if it is recognized that the chapels are primarily concerned to maintain their control of earnings and employment. The one advantage the different types of comprehensive agreements had in common was the improvement in the stability of earnings. Earnings which previously had fluctuated weekly were now averaged over the income tax year or half-year. At the time the chapels agreed to reduce the number of jobs there was little or no unemployment. Indeed, many of the jobs reduced were 'ghosts'. Comprehensive agreements also provided an opportunity to increase the number of regular jobs which was another objective to be achieved when there was no unemployment. A reduction in the number of jobs also seemed to be the only way of maintaining real standards in the face of the managements which wished to introduce new plant or equipment, or

---

breaks during the night when the presses were shut down. To meet increases in circulation, the management decided to introduce continuous running, thereby cutting out the meal breaks. It was therefore agreed that the workers were entitled to a 'blow'. Technological change was also a factor: changes in the ink-ducts and spindles on the presses reduced the workload of the Oiler, allowing more time for 'blows'.

a government policy which required workers to justify increases in earnings. Unemployment in the printing industry required an about-turn in this thinking. The pressing need now was to maintain and, if possible, increase the number of jobs.

Development of Payment by Task

How then can the findings in Chapters 2, 3 and 4 be explained? The key is the system of payment by task which has developed to meet a need to control the impact of the discontinuities in production on working arrangements. The argument can best be put as follows. Most of the occupations in the production and maintenance departments in Fleet Street, like time workers in other industries, are paid for the hours of attendance. However, unlike the piece worker, there is a lack of precision in the relationship between payment and effort.[23] To quote Behrend:

> The reason for this lack of precision (in the employment contract) is uncertainty. The employer cannot define tasks clearly in advance. He needs flexibility to adjust to changing conditions. Thus, what the employer purchases is not a given series of services but a supply of effort for performing particular types of services involving changing work assignments. He cannot define beforehand the exact nature of these assignments, nor how often and how quickly the same tasks will have to be performed.[24]

Legally, it is assumed that the time worker will carry out all the reasonable instructions of his employer; in entering into a contract of employment, in effect, he signs a blank cheque.[25] Problems arise because it is likely that the employer and the worker will hold different notions about what constitutes a fair day's work. In stable situations few of these problems may arise in practice. In the words of W. Baldamus, 'the relevant expectations tend to become standardised; everybody is familiar with the prevailing notions of effort and earnings customary in that situation.'[26] In a situation of rapid change these problems may arise daily. As the previous section

23. To contrast the difference between payment by time and payment by results, the NBPI has suggested the following definition for the latter: 'any system under which payment is related to factors in a worker's performance other than time spent at his employer's disposal'. NBPI Report No. 65, *Payment by Results Systems*, Cmnd. 3627 (London: HMSO, 1968), p. 3.
24. 'A Fair Day's Work', *Scottish Journal of Political Economy* (1961), p. 103.
25. See the argument in H. A. Simon, *Models of Men* (New York: J. Wiley, 1957), ch. 11.
26. 'The Relationship between Wage and Effort', *Journal of Industrial Economics* (July 1957), p. 196.

has already pointed out, in Fleet Street changes in the product and fluctuations in the level of activity in the product market are such that workers are obliged to seek some control over the payment system; for without this control the managements would be free to determine what constitutes a fair day's work. Yet these changes and fluctuations also provide workers with the opportunity to gain control, simply and effectively, by forcing the managements to negotiate their co-operation whenever there is a need to alter working arrangements.[27] The result is a system of payment by task. As one industrial relations manager has put it: 'We pay the basic rate to get the men to come to the office. Then we have to pay them for everything they do!'

Once it is recognized that there is a system of payment by task, the large number and variety of components of pay described in Chapter 4 no longer pose a problem. It also becomes possible to explain the differences and changes in earnings which Chapter 7 has already established were associated with differences and changes in page sizes. To quote a simple example, the Permanent Time Hands in most offices receive payments, usually in the form of hours of overtime, which are related to the page sizes of the newspapers. It might be two hours' overtime for a 24pp. issue, three hours for a 32pp. issue, and four hours for a 48pp. issue. Other things being equal, then, it stands to reason that earnings will be higher the more 48pp. issues there are. The same is true of many of the other components of pay described in Chapter 4, including the extras negotiated by the NPA and the trade unions.

Comparability

In the absence of effective competition in the labour market, it

27. Of course, it could be said that this insistence on mutuality underpins the idea of 'job property rights' believed by H. A. Turner *et al.* to be one of the two ideas which best express the changes in the expectations of manual workers in the post-war period — the other being the idea of 'fair comparison'. For example, of the idea of 'job property rights' they write: 'In manual workers' terms, it extends not merely to the sense that operatives should not be turned off en masse when it is no longer profitable to employ them, or that the individual worker should not be deprived of his property rights established by service without appeal from the decision of management which now finds his presence undesirable; it also includes the idea of rights to a particular job at a particular place, and may extend to the right to consultation in anything which may affect the future of his "property".' *Labour Relations in the Motor Industry* (London: Allen and Unwin, 1968), p. 337.

might be expected that comparisons between chapels would play an important part in explaining the levels of payments and earnings which result from the process described above. In practice, it could be said that each chapel has three possible reference groups within Fleet Street with which to compare itself.[28] First, there are the members of other chapels in the same department who, for convenience, will be referred to as Group A. They are employed by the same company. They work on the same newspaper. Physical contact is close; they work alongside one another, talk to each other, and develop friendships. They experience changes in the product and changes in the level of activity in the product market in very much the same ways. In many departments in Fleet Street, the members of the different chapels stand in relation to each other as journeyman and assistant. Traditional differentials are likely to be important. The journeyman will be anxious to protect his status as well as his material standard, believing that if he fails to defend the differential, he is also failing in his duties as a member of the union.[29] Secondly, there are the members of chapels in other

28. To quote R. Hyman, 'The notion of reference group is employed in sociology and social psychology to denote the source of a frame of reference which structures an individual's attitudes or actions.' *Social Values and Industrial Relations: A Study of Fairness and Inequality*, forthcoming. But it is also important to be aware of the three different types of reference groups. First, there is the 'membership' reference group, which is 'the particular role a person has in mind in the context of the inequality which he feels'. Second, there is the 'comparative' reference group which is the group whose situation or attributes a person contrasts with his own. Thirdly, there is the 'normative' reference group from which a person takes his standards. See W. G. Runciman, *Relative Deprivation and Social Justice* (London: Routledge & Kegan Paul, 1966), ch. 2. Given the levels of earnings in Fleet Street, it might be thought that the study was on safe ground in excluding comparisons outside Fleet Street. However, the fact that increases in earnings in the period 1967 to 1970 were greater than in the period 1961 to 1964, when there was nothing exceptional about the increase in page sizes, might be explained by the comparisons which were made with the *percentage increase* in wage rates and earnings in other industries. The end of the period, it will be remembered, witnessed the famous 'wages explosion' following the relaxation of the Labour Government's prices and incomes policy.

29. In discussing the strength of craft traditions, Flanders makes the point that: 'for craftsmen . . . they are matters of principle, to fail to defend them is to fail in one's duties as a member of the group . . .' He also adds something, borrowed from his experience at Esso, Fawley, which is extremely relevant to the situation in Fleet Street: 'Even when "the skill gap between craftsmen and non-craftsmen becomes largely notional, or could be easily crossed by a fairly brief period of training" ', as it could in most production departments in Fleet Street, ' ". . . the craft remains a craft" provided union members can successfully defend the work preserve against trespass. "Indeed the more notional the skill gap becomes" ',

departments in the same office, who will be referred to as Group B. They are employed by the same company. They work on the same newspaper. Physical contact is likely to be less than with Group A. They experience the same changes in the product and the level of activity in the product market, but the precise impact will be different. Traditional differentials are not likely to be as important as with Group A, though still important. Thirdly, there are workers in the same occupation in other offices who will be referred to as Group C. They are employed by different companies. They work on different newspapers. Physical contact is likely to be less than with Group A but still close because of the geographical concentration and the patterns of working. The manufacturing process is very similar from office to office, but changes in the product and changes in the level of activity in the product market will be different. The common occupation and shared traditions are the bond in this case; failure to negotiate what has been gained by the members in other offices would be letting the side down.

The three groups, then, are likely to have a significant influence which would help to explain why there are similarities and differences between the offices. But more can be done. By using a form of analysis of variance, it can be established whether earnings tended to move more in line with the office (Groups A and B) or the occupation (Group C).[30] The increase in earnings of workers in each occupation in each office was subtracted from the increase in

---

as in the machine and reading departments in Fleet Street. ' "the greater the significance of their demarcation practices to the craftsmen" for they are then more like a sea wall which stands between the inhabitants of the island and total flood!' A. Flanders, 'Trade Unions and the Force of Tradition', in *Management and Trade Unions. loc. cit.*, pp. 285-6. See also A. Flanders, *The Fawley Productivity Agreements* (London: Faber and Faber, 1964), p. 216.

30. This technique is used by D. I. MacKay *et al., Labour Markets Under Different Employment Conditions* (London: Allen and Unwin, 1971), pp. 124-5. To calculate the first total (Vi), the following formula was used:

$$V_1 = \sum_{j=1}^{n} [(x_{fj} - x_{wj})^2 + (x_{tj} - x_{wj})^2 + (x_{lj} - x_{wj})^2]$$

where X_{fj}, X_{tj}, and X_{wj} represent the percentage changes in the average weekly earnings of Permanent Time Hands. Linotype Operators. Piece Case Hands etc. and 'All Occupations' in the jth office.

To calculate the second total (Vii). the formula was:

$$V_2 = \sum_{j=1}^{n} [(x_{fj} - \bar{x}_f)^2 + (x_{tj} - \bar{x}_t)^2 + (x_{tj} - \bar{x}_l)^2]$$

earnings of workers in 'All Occupations' in that office. In each case the result was squared and added together to form a grand total. The same formula was then used to establish the amount by which the increases in earnings of workers in each occupation in each office departed from the increases in earnings in that occupation in 'All Offices'. If the first grand total is less than the second, this suggests that earnings moved more in line with those of other occupations in the same office. If the second is less, this suggests that earnings moved more in line with those of workers in the same occupation in other offices.

For each office the mean square deviation (MSD) of the two measures was calculated for the periods 1961 to 1964, 1964 to 1967, and 1967 to 1970. The aggregate MSD for all offices is shown in Table 8.3. Column 1 gives the MSD from office average earnings increases and column 2 the MSD from occupation average earnings increase. Column 3 expresses the first as a percentage of the second. Column 4 gives the percentage of offices for which the MSD from the office average increase is greater than the MSD from the occupation average. Column 4, it should be pointed out, has been worked out on a disaggregated basis.

It will be seen that the column 2 figure is smaller than the column 1 figure for the period 1961 to 1964, which suggests that earnings tended to move more in line with the occupation than the office in this period. In the following periods, however, the influence of the office would appear to have taken over — the column 1 figure is smaller in both cases — and, from column 4, would appear to have done so in the majority of offices. [31]

But how can the difference of emphasis be fitted into the

---

where X_f, X_t, and X_l represent the percentage changes in average weekly earnings in all offices for Permanent Time Hands, Linotype Operators, Piece Case Hands etc.

Twenty of the twenty-five occupations included in the study formed the basis of the totals shown in Table 8.2. Five of the occupations were omitted because some offices failed to make a return in 1970. However, there is no reason to believe that their omission makes any material difference to the findings presented in the tables; the inclusion of these five occupations for the periods 1961 to 1964 and 1964 to 1967, for example, did not disturb the balance of the totals.

31. MacKay *et al.* found that in both Birmingham and Glasgow the results of the analysis of variance supported the 'view that changes in earnings are dependent upon economic conditions in the plant rather than on the occupation of the worker'. *op. cit.*, p. 125.

argument? There is one very good reason for expecting that comparisons with workers in the same occupation in other offices (Group C) would be the dominant influence in the earlier period: the

TABLE 8.3

ANALYSIS OF VARIANCE: COMPARISON OF MEAN SQUARE DEVIATION (MSD) OF EARNINGS INCREASES OF INDIVIDUAL OFFICE-OCCUPATION GROUPS FROM THE AVERAGE EARNINGS INCREASE OF, RESPECTIVELY, THEIR OFFICES AND THEIR OCCUPATIONS

Each year is represented by its October figure	MSD of all office-occupation earnings increases from earnings increase of their own office	MSD of all office-occupation earnings from earnings increase of their own occupation	Column 1 as a percentage of column 2	Percentage of offices for which 1 is greater than 2
	(1)	(2)	(3)	(4)
	%	%	%	%
1961 - 1964	146.2	136.6	107.0	20
1964 - 1967	165.8	227.0	73.0	50
1967 - 1970	235.1	297.2	73.2	60

nature of the information about pay. With a system of payment by task, it was much easier to make comparisons between the components of pay in the different offices than between earnings which were constantly changing. Also, by insisting on the same components of pay, the notion of 'a rate for the job' could still be upheld. As one management explained in its written evidence to the Royal Commission on the Press, 1961-2:

Once accepted in one office these practices tend to become standard for the industry. Furthermore, where additional payments are made in one house, these are frequently used as a precedent for an application for similar payments in other houses, refusal of which may lead to difficulties.[32]

By contrast, differences in the manufacturing process between departments made it extremely difficult to justify comparisons with the components of pay of chapels in other departments in the same office (Group B). Comparisons with the earnings of these chapels

32. Royal Commission on the Press, 1961-2, *Documentary Evidence*, Cmnd. 1812-4 (London: HMSO, 1962), p. 70.

were also ruled out because these too were constantly changing. The only comparisons which could be made within the office were with other chapels in the same department (Group A), which helps to explain the similarities within departments noted in Chapters 2 and 3.

This situation changed in the mid-1960s. As Chapter 10 will argue in greater detail, the managements experienced growing pressure to control costs. This, together with the impetus provided by the Labour Government's incomes policy, forced them to negotiate comprehensive agreements. Now, as Chapter 4 has already pointed out, one important consequence of the negotiation of these agreements was the consolidation of the components of pay into a single 'comprehensive' or 'equated' weekly rate which is calculated over the income tax year or half-year. For the first time the earnings of other chapels within the same office were made explicit, revealing in some cases the large differences in earnings which had developed over the years when the levels of earnings had been obscure. While the chapels continued to make comparisons between offices, their attention was inevitably drawn to the 'comprehensive' or 'equated' weekly rates of other chapels in the same office. The result was an intensification of the use of comparisons within the offices which helps to explain the narrowing in occupational differentials.

Special Cases

The situation in the maintenance departments in which the occupations received above-average increases in earnings is a very good example of what happened. For many years there had been attempts on the part of members of the two maintenance unions to disassociate themselves from the industry negotiations of the printing unions and to establish a separate identity. Their strike in 1955 is perhaps the best-known example.[33] They also expressed the

33. The strike by Engineers and Electricians which lasted some four weeks began at the end of March 1955. With the three-year agreements negotiated in 1951 coming to an end in October 1954, the NPA had commenced negotiations with the printing unions under the aegis of the PKTF. Approached by the two maintenance unions, the NPA made similar offers to the Engineers and Electricians which were rejected. The Engineers and Electricians argued that they wanted their claims considered on their merits and were not prepared to follow automatically the settlements reached with the printing unions. This was

fear at the time of the strike and in subsequent negotiations that the practice of the printing chapels in negotiating a large number of components of pay had undermined the structure of industry basic rates. There can be little doubt that both Engineers and Electricians took the opportunity provided by the negotiations of comprehensive agreements to put themselves out in front in what they thought to be their rightful place.

Comparisons between Engineers and Electricians provided yet another dynamic, especially following the negotiation of comprehensive agreements. In the past Engineers had tended to opt for a pattern of working involving days or nights, whereas the Electricians preferred a pattern of rotating shifts. The result was that Engineers worked or were 'paid for' a number of hours of overtime far in excess of the Electricians. The latter tolerated this situation until the negotiation of comprehensive agreements which reduced the hours of workers in both occupations to the basic working week without any loss of earnings. Then they began to insist on parity with the Engineers. There was no longer any justification for the large differences in earnings, they argued, since they were paid the same industry basic rate and worked the same basic hours. Forced to concede their claims in full or in part, the managements then faced claims from the Engineers who wanted to know why the Electricians were receiving such large increases in earnings without making the fundamental change in working arrangements which they had agreed. The spiral which developed was given further impetus by the Engineers' Assistants. They inevitably compared themselves with the Engineers, and in some cases their earnings came perilously close to those of the Electricians.

There was another development in the mid-1960s which helps to explain the growing importance of comparisons within the offices. The amalgamation of the LTS and the TA in 1964 to form the NGA, and the subsequent transfer of engagements of the ACP and NUPT in 1966 and the NSES in 1967 had two important consequences. First, there was the fact of amalgamation itself: the different occupations were encouraged to believe that the new union would seek greater equality among its members and, some hoped, a single

---

essentially the issue on which the strike took place, leading to the setting up of a Court of Inquiry. For further details of the background to the strike, see *Report of a Court of Inquiry into a dispute between members of the NPA and members of the AEU and ETU*, Cmnd. 9439 (London: HMSO, 1955).

craft rate. Secondly, the NGA amalgamation also led in a number of offices to the setting up of an Imperial NGA Chapel. Although individual chapels still retained their autonomy and in some cases Machine Managers and Stereotypers remained outside, the Imperial FOC began to take part in negotiations affecting individual chapels. Both consequences help to explain the above-average increases in the earnings of Permanent Time Hands and Readers. The unfavourable comparison between the earnings of the Permanent Time Hands, on the one hand, and the Linotype Operators and Piece Case Hands, who are both paid by results, on the other, had posed problems for many years. For example, there were special difficulties in absorbing amounts from the cost of living bonus so that Linotype Operators and Piece Case Hands did not receive a disproportionate amount.[34] But the comparison did not stop here. Readers compared themselves with the Permanent Time Hands because they shared the same industry basic rate and extras. Wireroom and Telephoto Operators who had previously been members of the NUPT joined in. The fact that they were not nearly so successful as the other occupations only added to their discontent with the new union.

The intensification of comparisons among the occupations in membership of the NGA also had an effect on workers in the other occupations in the composing and reading departments who are members of the RIRMA branch of NATSOPA. In each case they compared themselves with members of the NGA who were higher paid. The signs that workers in these occupations were dissatisfied with the position in the internal pay structures were unmistakeable. RIRMA branch officers campaigned vigorously to improve this position in negotiations with the NPA and the individual managements.[35] Two closely related themes appear in the

34. In 1955 the LSC took the unprecedented step of deducting 45p. from the earnings of the piece workers and transferring it to the industry basic rates of the Permanent Time Hands to form the so-called 'allocated' rate. Each time the NPA and the unions attempted to reflect the absorption of 30p. into the London Scale of Prices in an equitable way, piece workers ended up with a larger sum of money than the Permanent Time Hands.
35. In 1960 the RIRMA branch of NATSOPA submitted 'domestic' claims on behalf of all the occupations in membership, with the exception of the Revisers. Its claims rejected, the branch repeated the exercise in1964 and was rewarded with increases for Engineers and Linotype Assistants and Photoprinters. In an attempt to improve the relative position of the Proofpullers, the branch transferred these members to the Printing Machine branch of SOGAT where

arguments used. First, RIRMA members felt themselves to be 'second-class citizens'; they argued that the distinction between 'craft' and 'non-craft' was outdated; there was, they said, a continuum of skills each of which should be rewarded according to its contribution. Secondly, they made comparisons with members of NATSOPA in the machine department who because of their superior organization had been able to secure relatively high earnings. The industry basic rates of RIRMA members, they argued, were derived from those of NATSOPA members in the machine department and yet there were considerable differences in earnings. There were also unfavourable comparisons with the Engineers' Assistants, who are members of the same chapel in some offices, and whose earnings had increased substantially, because of the association with the Engineers and Electricians' Assistants.

It now becomes clear why the negotiation of comprehensive agreements had such a dramatic effect on the internal pay structures. But there is one final observation to be made. To be successful in closing differentials, lower-paid workers had to have at least the tacit co-operation of the higher paid. If they had not, then the latter would have sought to restore the differential. In this situation the size and measure of the differential were significant. A comparison between the machine and reading departments will illustrate. Chapter 3 found that there was little change in the percentage differentials in the machine department but a marked narrowing in the reading departments. Differentials in the machine department were already much closer than in the reading department. Whereas there was some room to manoeuvre in the latter department before members of the NGA were likely to react, this was not the case in the machine department, as the management of the *Daily Mirror* found to its cost. It was also extremely rare for differentials in the reading department to narrow in absolute terms, which suggests that the members of the NGA were not prepared to accept that any single component of pay should be less than that which was negotiated with members of NATSOPA.

---

they joined the apprentice-trained Pressmen whose name they subsequently adopted. 'Copyholders' also became 'Copyreaders' during this period — another attempt to improve status. Finally, the branch was active in seeking fixed differentials with members of the NGA in negotiations with the managements about comprehensive agreements.

All this confirms that the attitudes and policies of the chapels were significant for the findings in Chapters 2, 3 and 4. The large number and variety of components of pay described in Chapter 4 are intelligible in the light of the development of a system of payment by task; and so too are the differences and changes in earnings noted in Chapters 2 and 3. The similarities between the offices can be explained by the comparisons with the components of pay in the different offices. Finally, the narrowing in differentials within the offices which was also noted in Chapter 3 can be explained by the attempts of a number of the occupations to improve their relative position in the internal pay structures, given the information made available by the negotiation of comprehensive agreements.

Chapter 9

The Trade Unions

The following trade unions had members in the production and maintenance departments of the newspaper offices in Fleet Street in 1961 and 1974 respectively:

1961	1974
London Typographical Society	
Association of Correctors of the Press	
National Union of Press Telegraphists	National Graphical Association
National Society of Electrotypers and Stereotypers	
Society of Lithographic Artists, Designers, Engravers and Process Workers	Society of Lithographic Artists, Designers, Engravers and Process Workers
National Society of Operative Printers and Assistants	National Society of Operative Printers, Graphical and Media Personnel
National Union of Printing, Bookbinding and Paper Workers	Society of Graphical and Allied Trades
Amalgamated Engineering Union	Amalgamated Union of Engineering Workers
Electrical Trade Union	Electrical, Electronic and Plumbing Trade Union

Both the LSC and the PMMTS, which amalgamated in 1955 to form the LTS, were London-based unions. The LSC with some 13,990 members organized Compositors within a radius of fifteen miles of

125

Charing Cross. The PMMTS had some 5,680 members, organizing Machine Managers within the same radius of the General Post Office. The TA, with which the LTS amalgamated in 1964 to form the NGA, was a Manchester-based union with some 52,600 members, organizing Compositors, Readers, and Machine Managers outside London in England and Wales.[1] The ACP was another London-based union with only 1,449 members, organizing Readers within a radius of fifteen miles of Charing Cross. The NUPT and the NSES were both national unions, the NUPT with 1,540 members and the NSES with 5,268 members.[2] The ASLP, which amalgamated with the NGA in 1969, had no members in the newspaper offices in Fleet Street and Manchester and the total number of members was approximately 12,400.

The union that resulted from these amalgamations, the NGA, had approximately 110,000 members in 1970. Its headquarters are in Bedford. It is also significant that the NGA has adopted the trade group principle, the occupational categories forming trade groups with national officers. Each trade group has a consultative committee which advises the Executive Council on matters affecting its members. The union is still in the process of re-organizing its branches, following the amalgamations. The London Region, which is the largest in numbers, covers the area which previously had come under the jurisdiction of the London-based unions. There is a 'News' committee which deals exclusively with the affairs of the members in Fleet Street.

SOGAT was formed as a result of the amalgamation of NATSOPA and the NUPB & PW in 1966, the two unions operating as separate divisions, Division 1 and Division A respectively, until the end of the period, by which time they had both gone their separate ways again, Division A retaining the title 'SOGAT'. NATSOPA has members in most sections of the printing industry, but the greater proportion is in newspapers, provincial as well as national. Starting as the Printers' Labourers' Union in 1889, it had gradually recruited most of the workers ignored by the craft unions in Fleet Street and Manchester, together with clerical and administrative workers. NATSOPA has three London branches. The London Machine Branch caters for all members in the machine

1. In Scotland these occupations are members of the STA.
2. The London branch of the NSES was a separately constituted union which enjoyed considerable autonomy from the national union.

departments; it had two full-time officials in 1970. The RIRMA branch, which also had two full-time officers, caters for the other members in the production and maintenance departments: Photoprinters, Revisers, Copyreaders, Linotype Assistants, Engineers' Assistants, Doormen, Firemen, Cleaners and Messengers. The Clerical, Executive and Administrative Branch looks after the interests of the clerical and administrative workers, enforcing membership to a very senior level in the newspaper offices.[3] It also had two full-time officials in 1970.

SOGAT, formerly the NUPB & PW, is the most broadly based of the printing unions, with members in newspapers, distribution, printing, paper and board-making. It is itself the product of a complex series of amalgamations, and had some 180,000 members at the time of the amalgamation with NATSOPA. The union has three branches with members in Fleet Street. The London Central Branch, the largest, caters for all the members in the publishing departments; in 1970 it had six full-time officers although not all of them were involved in the affairs of Fleet Street. The Printing Machine Branch has relatively few members in Fleet Street, only a handful until 1967 and the transfer of Proof-pullers from the RIRMA branch of NATSOPA; it had two full-time officers in 1970. The third branch looks after the interests of the Circulation Representatives.

SLADE is another national union which had approximately 15,000 members in 1970. In Fleet Street its members are to be found in the process department, where they make the picture blocks. In many sections of the printing industry its members are increasingly involved in the plate-making process. The London branch had four full-time officers in 1970.

Little need be said in this study about the AEUW and the EEPTU. Members of the AUEW in Fleet Street come under the London District, but in practice are the special responsibility of the Divisional Organizer. There is also a Press branch with a lay secretary. Similarly the Area Secretary has special responsibility for the members of the EEPTU and again there is a Press branch with a lay secretary.

There are two reasons for giving separate attention to the trade

3. Only senior managers and their secretaries are exempt from compulsory membership. There is an agreement between the NPA and the branch which provides for the setting up of an *ad hoc* committee to consider contested cases.

unions. First, given that the trade unions are responsible for negotiating revisions to the industry rates, it is important to establish why were there no major changes in the structure of these rates despite the disputes in 1968 and 1970,[4] and despite the setting up of the Joint Board for the National Newspaper Industry and the National Newspaper Steering Group. Secondly, the trade unions may seek to influence the negotiations between the managements and chapels, and it is important to know what form this takes and what effect, if any, this had.

The Trade Unions and the Industry Basic Rates

The main reason for the absence of major changes in the structure of the industry basic rates, as Chapter 11 will also argue, was the inability of the trade unions to co-operate with one another. As a result, it was impossible at times for them to negotiate collectively with the NPA, despite widespread agreement that the gap between the industry basic rates and earnings should be closed, and it was equally impossible for the NPA to treat one union more favourably than the others.

The amalgamations described in the previous section are important for the understanding of the conflict of interests between the unions. The NGA amalgamation, for example, represented an attempt on the part of craft unions which were geographically based or restricted to a single occupation to protect the status of their members. In both cases dwindling numbers were a key factor in overcoming years of separate existence. Inevitably NATSOPA and SOGAT were seen as major threats. These two, which had been forced by the exclusiveness of the craft unions to adopt a more open recruitment policy, were equally anxious to take advantage of technological change to promote the interests of their members.

There were two main areas of conflict. One was jurisdictional. Technological change in the machine department occasioned numerous demarcation disputes between members of the NGA and NATSOPA; in Fleet Street, for example, there were a number of disputes during the period. The position of the two unions can best be illustrated by studying their arguments before the Cameron Court of Inquiry set up to investigate disputes at Southwark Offset in

4. These disputes are discussed in Appendices II and III.

London and the Co-operative Press in Manchester.[5] The NGA argued that the disputes had been caused by an overt act of aggression by NATSOPA for which no justification had been offered; the union could not accept NATSOPA's claim to share the control of web-offset presses without restricting the employment opportunities of its members. NATSOPA denied that it was challenging the jurisdiction of the craft unions. On the other hand, it could not tolerate the situation in which its members were refused promotion opportunities no matter how great their experience might be.

In Fleet Street there was also conflict over differentials and Appendix I describes one such dispute. NATSOPA and SOGAT had taken the initiative in negotiating comprehensive agreements involving a reduction in the number of jobs. The NGA had held back. Many members were opposed in principle. More importantly, they believed that the negotiation of comprehensive agreements would inevitably disturb differentials between themselves and the members of the other two unions; for it was firmly believed by members of the NGA that the members of these unions had proportionately more jobs to 'sell'.

Indirectly, the NGA amalgamation and the amalgamation of NATSOPA and the NUPB & PW to form SOGAT were also a cause of animosity. These amalgamations were regarded as a necessary stage in the formation of one single union for the printing industry, and yet for much of the period with which this study is concerned they only made the situation worse. It was as if there were two power blocks, each justifying its existence by reference to the other.

The amalgamations were also significant because they consumed the greater part of the time of full-time officers and the Executives of the unions. There were many problems of digestion. The siting of the NGA headquarters in Bedford was no accident, being an attempt to balance the interests of the Manchester-based TA with the London-based LTS. There were also rumblings of discontent among members of the former NUPT. The amalgamation of NATSOPA and the NUPB & PW was also beginning to break up, largely as a

5. See *Report of a Court of Inquiry into the problems caused by the introduction of web-offset machines into the printing industry, and the problems arising from the introduction of other modern printing techniques and the arrangements which should be adopted within the industry for dealing with them*, Cmnd. 3184 (London: HMSO, 1967).

result of animosities among the leaderships of the two divisions.[6]

It should come as no surprise to learn that in this situation the authority of the PKTF waned rapidly. The refusal of the printing unions to allow the two maintenance unions to join was a missed opportunity.[7] Then, the NGA and SOGAT amalgamations made it all but impossible for the PKTF to function. After all, it was hardly realistic for Federation officials to seek to mediate in disputes between the two unions which supplied the president and vice-president respectively!

Influence on Negotiations between Managements and Chapels

The trade unions naturally influence negotiations between the managements and chapels through the industry agreements. The most significant agreements during this period were the ones which laid down the guidelines for the negotiation of comprehensive agreements. But it remains to be seen if the unions influenced the outcome of these negotiations and, if so, what effect this had.

At first sight, there seems to be a conflict of interest. The chapels are jealous of their autonomy and yet most of the branches in London stipulate that agreements negotiated by the managements and chapels should be ratified by the branch committee. This ruling applies in every case to comprehensive agreements. Branch officials are usually actively involved in the final stages of the negotiations and almost invariably their signature will be on the agreement; in

6.   The story of the break-up of NATSOPA and the NUPB & PW has yet to be told. It is extremely complicated and only the briefest of details will be given here. Underlying the legal wranglings, there would seem to be two basic issues. One was a straightforward personality clash between the leaders of the two divisions. A number of Division A officials, among them those who stood to lose most from the amalgamation, rebelled against what they regarded as a takeover by the smaller, financially weaker, union. The other issue was closely related. Ever since the days of George Isaacs, the formal power in NATSOPA had rested with the general secretary and the executive. In the NUPB & PW the situation was different. The branches enjoyed considerable autonomy, having, for example, control over their own finances. Proposals to reduce this autonomy in the amalgamated union naturally confirmed the worst suspicions of some Division A officials. So began the wrangle about the intention of the original instrument of amalgamation, which eventually led Division 1 to withdraw.

7.   See their evidence in *Report of a Court of Inquiry into a dispute between members of the NPA and members of the AEU and ETU,* Cmnd. 9439 (London: HMSO, 1955).

some cases the agreement is between the management and the branch. In practice, however, there is very little conflict. To all intents and purposes, the chapels in Fleet Street *are* the branch. Many FOCs sit on the branch committee and have a powerful voice in determining the policies. Many of the full-time officers are ex-FOCs from Fleet Street, the size of the chapels in Fleet Street giving them a disproportionate influence in elections. So full-time officials are as much chapel officials as those formally elected at chapel meetings. Another point is that the weakness of the managements, as already suggested, renders many full-time officers impotent when disagreements with the policies of a chapel arise.

The influence of the trade unions on the outcome of the negotiations between the managements and chapels was significant in two respects for the findings in Chapters 2, 3 and 4. First of all, they encouraged the use of comparisons by providing the chapels with an opportunity to discuss and exchange information about the situation in the different offices. But there is one important difference between the unions and the NPA in this respect. The managements are often embarrassed by concessions made in other offices. It is extremely rare for one chapel to embarrass other chapels in the union in the same way. Chapel officials are unlikely to be ignorant of branch policy in a given area and can quickly sound out opinion if there is as yet no policy. But there is still a safeguard if these informal processes break down. If a chapel should make a concession which others in the union believe to be embarrassing to their interests, it can be vetoed by the branch committee, and there is very little the management can do. Contrast this with the position of the NPA. If one of the managements makes an embarrassing concession it is hardly realistic for the NPA to exercise a veto. If it does and the chapel takes industrial action, there is very little the NPA can do.

Secondly, a number of the findings in Chapters 2 and 3 conform to explicit policies of the branches, suggesting that the influence of the trade unions was not without more positive effect. Chapter 8 has already pointed out that the RIRMA branch of NATSOPA was particularly active in seeking to improve the position of its members in the pay structure. Not only did it have some success in negotiations with the NPA but also in negotiations with the managements; for if the attempt to secure fixed differentials with members of the NGA and the AUEW was unsuccessful, it undoubtedly helped to narrow their differential over members of RIRMA. The two maintenance unions are another interesting case. The tendency for the inter-office differentials to narrow in the period 1967 to 1970 may be attributed to a policy of lifting the earnings of the members in lower paying offices up to those in the higher paying offices. Similarly, the exceptional increases in the earnings of Electricians may be attributed to a policy of achieving parity with Engineers following the negotiation of comprehensive agreements. Yet another example of the influence of the unions is their opposition to further reductions in the number of jobs in view of the unemployment among members in the printing industry towards the end of the period. This helps to explain why no office was able to achieve a reduction in *total* production wages in the period 1967 to 1970.

Chapter 10

The Managements

Chapter 1 has already given details of the companies which publish the newspapers in Fleet Street. The managements in these companies are defined throughout this study as 'a particular group of people, those legally empowered to represent the owners of the business'.[1] Two problems have to be faced, however, despite the simplicity of this definition. The first is shared by all students of management. Management is not a single group of people; it is made up of a number of 'differing and sometimes contending groups'.[2] The EIU Report, for example, suggested that the 'most striking feature about the managements in Fleet Street is their dominance by a small number of proprietors'.[3] In using proprietor to describe 'the dominant personality in the organisation',[4] it follows common usage in Fleet Street. But the term also has a firm basis in fact: in seven of the nine companies publishing newspapers in Fleet Street the proprietor and members of his family are either the majority or largest single shareholder, or the controlling interest of a trust.[5] The other groups which must be considered are the editors, the advertising directors, the circulation managers, the industrial relations managers, and the overseers. The second problem arises because this chapter makes statements about these different groups of managers without distinguishing between the

1. N. W. Chamberlain and J. Kuhn, *Collective Bargaining* (2nd ed., New York: McGraw Hill, 1965), p. 210.
2. *ibid.*, p. 217.
3. EIU Report, p. 52. Over the years many of these proprietors have become household names. The following is only a selection: Beaverbrook, Kemsley, Murdoch, Northcliffe, Riddel, Rothermere, Scott, Southwood, Thomson.
4. *ibid.*, p. 52.
5. The two companies without a proprietor in the legal sense are The Financial Times Ltd and IPC Newspapers Ltd. Trusts control the *Guardian* and the *Observer*.

offices. The EIU Report pointed out that it was dangerous to generalize in this way in any industry but particularly hazardous in Fleet Street because of the differences in management philosophies.[6] For better or worse, this chapter makes use of the EIU's own apology; when 'general statements are made', 'they are used to illustrate a predominant feature of the industry, in the full knowledge that a specific example can almost certainly be found to disprove any general statement'.[7]

Goals and Constraints

Because the proprietor is the 'dominant personality' in most of the companies which publish the newspapers, his goals and constraints inevitably set the pattern for the other groups of managers who have to be considered. This is especially true of such senior managers as the managing director or general manager and, to all intents and purposes, there is no reason to distinguish them from the proprietor. Even those companies which do not have a proprietor in the strict sense of the word are not totally immune to their influence because of the competition; also, it is possible to identify a dominant personality in these companies who acts very much like a proprietor.

The evidence suggests one inescapable conclusion: few, if any, of the proprietors see profitability as their sole or primary goal. The EIU Report, for example, suggested that:

The professional manager looks upon profits as a yard stick of efficiency and success, but some newspaper proprietors often subordinate profitability to other considerations. Thus some unprofitable newspapers are subsidised by other interests, or profits are substantially lower than could be achieved by more commercial management.[8]

The economic situation of the newspapers has already been discussed in Chapter 7. In the period 1961 to 1966, for example, only three out of eight daily newspapers were making profits and a number of the remainder made substantial losses. Some of the newspapers have to be supported by other newspapers within the company, one example being the *Guardian* which is subsidized by the profits from the *Manchester Evening News*.[9] Similarly, it has

6. p. 52.
7. *ibid*.
8. p. 53.
9. For the origins of the Scott Trust see David Ayerst, 'The Owning of a

been suggested that a number hold shares in Independent Broadcasting Authority companies in order to 'defend themselves against the loss of advertising revenue to television and to sustain their newspapers with profits from TV'.[10]

One proprietor has admitted that the motives of those who publish the newspapers may appear 'mixed and confused'.[11] However, he does offer his own views on why they continue to do so despite the lack of profitability:

It probably has something to do with the fact that all newspapers in some degree, and serious newspapers to a high degree, are a part of politics. In spite of radio and television, they still perform a significant political role, and it is this fact more than any other that makes those who control newspapers unwilling to close them down. [12]

Two possible motives are implicit in this statement. A proprietor may see his newspaper as a medium for propagating his own political views and opinions, though few these days would readily admit to such a motive. Or a proprietor may believe that he is performing a public service by helping to maintain the existing number of newspapers. In doing so, he may share the concern of those responsible for drafting the terms of reference of the Royal Commission on the Press, 1961-2, 'having regard to the importance, in the public interest, of the accurate presentation of news and the free expression of opinion'.[13]

Some of the proprietors may be motivated by family tradition. Five of the companies which publish newspapers in Fleet Street are second or third generation family firms, and the comments of Sadler and Barry in a recent study in the printing industry are relevant: 'The family business is seen not only as an economic unit, providing the family with a source of income but also as a field of endeavour or service within which are to be found opportunities for achievement, matching the achievements of the past.'[14] A proprietor may therefore pursue a particular editorial policy because of family

Newspaper', the *Guardian*, 1 Jan. 1973.

10. R. Eglin and D. Haworth, the *Observer*, 3 May 1970. A number of the companies which publish national newspapers also have wide-ranging interests outside newspapers and television. For details see *National Newspaper Industry* (Labour Research Department, 1972).

11. David Astor, the *Observer*, 26 Sept. 1971.

12. *ibid.*

13. Terms of reference of the Royal Commission on the Press, 1961-2.

14. P. J. Sadler and B. A. Barry, *Organisational Development* (London: Longmans, Green, 1970), p. 33.

sentiment. Or he may refuse to close a newspaper which is making substantial losses because it was his father's or grandfather's prize possession.

In some cases the motives of the proprietors may not be as rational as this discussion suggests. The exercise of 'charismatic' or 'traditional' authority may itself offer intrinsic satisfaction far outweighing those associated with the goals already discussed. To quote Sadler and Barry again, 'the role of the entrepreneur involves satisfaction of a kind associated with games and sports — risk-taking, meeting challenges and problem solving'.[15]

No matter the goals a proprietor sets himself, the one challenge which he cannot ignore is the competition of the other newspapers. Competition between the newspapers, as Chapter 7 has already pointed out, is intense. In particular, the newspapers within the same categories are to all intents and purposes direct substitutes for each other, so that every reader or advertiser gained by one newspaper is likely to represent a loss for the others. It is hardly surprising, then, that an initiative taken by one newspaper in the product market is almost automatically followed by others within the same category. They feel that they simply dare not take the risk of being left behind. But it is not only the economic argument which is important. The other goals may be paramount. A proprietor may be in competition with his fellow proprietors for the influence of his newspaper. The exclusive story and the definitive leader column — these offer intrinsic satisfactions irrespective of any longer-term economic significance. In short, to do better than one's competitors becomes an end in itself. Similarly, the competition from the other media imposes constraints. In spite of the attempt of the proprietor quoted above to reassure himself about the essentiality of newspapers, there is little doubt that television, in particular, has proved a powerful competitor.

The second group of managers which has to be considered is that of the editors.[16] They form a key group. As the EIU Report pointed out: 'The editorial content of a newspaper is largely responsible for the success or failure of that newspaper . . . possibly brilliant editorial can carry poor management, whereas brilliant manage-

15. *ibid.*, p. 35.
16. The term 'editor' is used here to describe those journalists who have some executive authority; it includes 'the' editor, the news editor, the features editor etc.

ment cannot carry poor editorial.'[17] But in doing this job the editors have to take decisions, often at a moment's notice, which have a direct impact on the working arrangements in the production and maintenance departments. In practice, the goals and constraints of the editors are very similar to those of the proprietors; indeed, in two offices the proprietor was editor-in-chief for much of the period. They must seek to maintain and, if possible, increase the number of readers in competition with the other newspapers. The rewards of success are great, involving both financial gain and public acclaim. Equally, the penalties of failure involve dismissal and redundancy. One result is that the editors are unlikely to be as aware as the proprietors of the cost constraint. The EIU Report noted a number of cases in which the editor had no budget or set the budget himself.[18]

Then there are the advertising directors. Like the editors, they take decisions which have an impact on the working arrangements in the production and maintenance departments. The amount of advertising, display or classified, affects the lay-out. The advertising directors' constraints are imposed by the competition not only with other newspapers but also with the other media. The proportion of total revenue which advertising revenue represents for many newspapers helps to explain their ever-increasing importance.

The circulation managers form the fourth group to be considered. Their job is to ensure that the newspaper is distributed in sufficient quantities and at the right time to the main-line railway terminals and to the wholesalers. The constraints may be measured in minutes, delays bringing complaints from the retailers and the possibility of loss sales to competitors.

It would be foolish to deny that costs do not impose any constraints on the goals of the proprietors and these other groups of managers. But from day to day they are of secondary importance. It

17. p. 57. Significantly, Woodward suggests that in unit production marketing is the first stage in the manufacturing process. Marketing 'sells' an idea which is then developed. Production is the final stage in the manufacturing process and works to firm orders only. In the case of newspapers, copy sales and readership develop over a period of time and depend on the ability of the editors. Apart from special sales drives or the coverage of particular events, the number of copies to be printed, the print order, is relatively constant and the page size depends on the amount of 'space' sold by the advertising department. See J. Woodward, *Industrial Organisation: Theory and Practice* (London: Oxford University Press, 1965), pp. 129ff.
18. p. 61.

is generally recognized that the newspapers in Fleet Street are faced, first and foremost, with a revenue problem;[19] and piecemeal additions to the wages bill, which is not the largest single item in total costs, can always be justified on the grounds of the need to attract and maintain readers and advertisers. In fact, it is no exaggeration to say that in the short term many proprietors publish their newspapers regardless of the costs.

By comparison, the damage which the chapels are able to inflict by taking industrial action is virtually incalculable. One proprietor, while ignoring the significance which this section has attached to competition in the product market, has given some impression of the frightening dilemma with which the managements are faced. In seeking to explain why they have 'silently given way' he argues:

the unique fragility of newspapers as a commodity makes them vulnerable to the slightest pressure.

If newspapers miss their trains, they cannot be put on ice, like food, and delivered the next day. If they are not delivered, the advertisers must be re-paid and all revenue is lost. So a short interruption of work, whether for a union meeting or because of a torn roll of paper requiring machines to be reset is enough to cause trains to be missed and therefore the loss of all revenue. Moreover, it is the fact that lost newspaper production over a number of days, weeks, or months, cannot be made up by greater subsequent production — as, for example, car manufacturers are, to some extent, able to do — that explains the inability of newspapers to survive prolonged shutdowns.

The extraordinary fragility is the whole explanation of the newspaper industry's peculiar behaviour.[20]

But paradoxically, the very weakness of their position helps to explain why the groups of managers mentioned above do not feel the chapels to be a serious constraint. The interference with what might be called their 'managerial prerogatives' is annoying and certainly time-consuming, but there is always an easy compromise, as long as the issue is one where co-operation can be bought with an increase in production wages or a concession which at least does not threaten the publication of the newspaper. Indeed, for the reason given earlier in this section, there seems little alternative. The managements in Fleet Street have no real sanctions. The ultimate sanction is to close the newspaper but for obvious reasons this is

19. This was the conclusion to which the Royal Commission on the Press and the NBPI both came.
20. David Astor, the *Observer*, 26 Sept. 1971. Of course, the fact that some of the companies which publish national newspapers do *not* have other interests makes them especially vulnerable to industrial action. It also reduces the possibility of concerted action by the NPA.

self-defeating. The famous 'One Stop. All Stop' policy which the NPA threatened to implement on several occasions during the period is essentially a mutual insurance policy.[21] It happens to be a retaliatory measure against a trade union whose members are taking industrial action. However, its principal aim is to protect the newspaper which is suffering the action from the competition of other newspapers — and this, more than anything else, explains why newspapers have remained in membership of the NPA.[22] But this is hardly a basis for firm action. In practice, the issue has to be one in which all newspapers believe their interests are at stake before they are prepared to close down. Only when an issue involves a dispute between two or more chapels or interference with the editorial contents of the newspaper do the goals of the proprietors and the other managers become seriously imperilled.[23] Issues such as these are the ones to which there is no easy compromise, the ones which lead to open conflict.

The industrial relations managers are the only group of managers who experience the chapels as a significant constraint.[24] They

21. The *One stop, All stop* policy required the newspapers to cease publication in the event of one newspaper being unable to publish because of industrial action. It was the subject of a formal agreement, the 'bond', until 1955 and the withdrawal of *The Times*. Thereafter, it survived as an informal understanding, the newspapers judging each issue on its merits. A further change of emphasis took place following a reprimand to the SDNS under the Restrictive Trade Practices Act. Subsequently, the policy took the form of threats to dismiss all members of the union taking industrial action. The policy has only been used on one occasion in recent years, in 1954 when the dispute between the PMMTS and NATSOPA over the transfer of the *Daily Sketch* to Associated Newspapers led to a one-night closure. The threat was made in 1966 in a dispute with NATSOPA and SOGAT over the night over day differential and in the *Daily Mirror* Managers' dispute in 1969. (See Appendix I.)
22. Following a dispute between the NPA and the NUJ over the negotiation of a 'Phase Three' settlement, the *Daily Mirror* and the *Sunday People* resigned from membership of the NPA in February 1974 in order to negotiate separate house agreements with NUJ chapels. It remains to be seen what effect, if any, the resignation of these three IPC newspapers has on the situation in Fleet Street.
23. The ban on interference with the editorial contents of the newspapers dates back to the General Strike and the refusal of *Daily Mail* chapels to print the leader on the miners' strike. In fact, there are surprisingly few examples of the chapels interfering with editorial contents. A famous example in recent years was the cartoon by Jak in the *Evening Standard* at the height of the Electricity Supply workers' dispute in 1970.
24. The term 'industrial relations' manager is used here to describe those managers who are responsible for day-to-day negotiations with the chapels. In some offices it may be the production manager and in others the staff relations manager; in two offices during the period it was the general manager or the assistant general manager.

139

have the difficult task of persuading the chapels to accept the decisions taken by the other managers which have an impact on the working arrangements in the production and maintenance departments. Significantly, the industrial relations managers are unable to implement these decisions unilaterally: they must first negotiate with the chapels. One of the managements in its evidence to the Royal Commission on the Press, 1961-2, frankly admitted:

When new plant was installed or some change was made in the programme of production such as an increase in paging or the bringing into use of a new building, agreement had to be reached in advance with the chapels representing the various sections of the staff who would be affected.[25]

It went on:

Manning and staffing, except in a few cases where provision is made in the NPA agreements, were arranged between the management of the *News Chronicle* and the *Star* and the appropriate chapels within the organisation. Conditions of work and additional payments for special duties were also arranged between managements and chapels.[26]

To make matters worse, the industrial relations managers have to negotiate separately with each and every one of the chapels whose members are affected. The members of the Royal Commission on Trade Unions questioned representatives of IPC Newspapers at some length about this practice. One of the representatives replied sadly: 'I think it would be a counsel of despair to regard it as inevitable but I think it is with us for some time yet.'[27] The representatives proceeded to explain why there was no alternative to separate negotiation with each chapel. They pointed to the effects of multi-unionism, especially prior to the NGA amalgamation. More significantly, they said that the chapels had the power to determine not only the scope but also the level and the unit of negotiations.

The industrial relations managers' job is not an easy one. They are always on the defensive. They are held responsible if any of the other groups of managers are unable to satisfy their goals because of opposition by the chapels. They also have to justify to these other groups the agreements they make with the chapels. Moreover, few proprietors are willing to delegate the necessary authority to them. They may be told, for example, to resist a chapel's claim because of

25. Royal Commission on the Press, 1961-2, *Documentary Evidence*. Cmnd. 1812-4 (London: HMSO, 1962), p. 148.
26. *ibid.*, p. 147.
27. Royal Commission on Trade Unions and Employers' Associations, *Minutes of Evidence*, 59 (London: HMSO, 1967), Question 9315.

the costs involved only to find that the proprietor or the managing director intervenes as soon as there is a serious threat to the production of the newspaper. In fact, it has not been unknown in some offices for the proprietor or managing director to encourage chapel officials to by-pass middle managers. In the words of one newspaper report:

Tense situations like this have bred a race of personnel men as skilled as anyone at 'fire-fighting'. Yet, at the same time, constant preoccupation with the short term situation has diverted attention from efforts to establish more long-sighted planning. 'What's the good of unveiling some grand new industrial relations plan to the board, if they turn round and ask, "Why isn't the paper coming out tonight?",' says one newspaper manager.[28]

The final group of managers to be considered are the overseers.[29] They are the first-line managers, and yet in practice their activities belie this function. In the majority of production departments, for example, the EIU Report noted that their function is technical rather than disciplinary.[30] Of the overseers in the machine department the Report concluded:

The degree of control by management is limited to machine allocation, technical work and quality control. Labour control is by chapel officers so there are in effect two managements, but only the chapel has direct authority. For example, it would not be possible for a supervisor to sack a man or apply disciplinary sanctions without first consulting the chapel.[31]

In many departments it is the FOC who draws up the work, overtime, and holiday rotas, and who notifies the branch when a vacancy occurs. In the machine and publishing departments it is the FOC who hires the labour and allocates it to the different tasks.

A recent example will illustrate what can happen in the case of discipline or dismissal. An Electrician returned to work after lunch rather drunk. He had an argument with the chief electrical overseer and abused him in front of other members cf the chapel. The overseer went to report the incident to the industrial relations manager but he was out. Next day the managing director learned of the incident and summarily dismissed the Electrician. Other Electricians working in the office at the time immediately stopped

28. R. Elgin and D. Haworth, *The Observer*, 3 May 1970.
29. The term 'overseer' is used to describe first-line managers. In the composing department the manager is known as the Printer and in the publishing department as the Publisher.
30. p. 105.
31. p. 176.

work until the managing director agreed to alter the penalty from dismissal to suspension. At a subsequent meeting the chapel officers stated categorically that the chapel would not allow the management to discipline the man further. They said that he had already been punished enough. He had been disciplined by the chapel who would not condone this type of conduct among its members: his drunkenness was a threat to safety; and his abuse of another member of the union was intolerable. The man had already apologized to the overseer and if any further discipline was required, he could be taken before the Branch Committee.

The reasons for this loss of authority are similar to those in other industries. The overseer is promoted from the shop-floor, but he has to remain a member of the trade union and is subject to its discipline.[32] The industrial relations manager himself is responsible for negotiations with the chapel, and the overseer has very little opportunity to affect earnings. Even the introduction of budgetary and cost controls has not had the desired effect because of the inability of the other groups of managers to forecast their requirements. In view of these pressures, it is hardly surprising that the overseers themselves have shown little appetite for conflict situations.

Attitudes and Policies towards Pay

Chapter 8 argued that the chapels determine the timing and the size of pay claims. The previous section has confirmed that they have the power to impose their demands. But the different groups of managers may still influence the negotiating process and the settlements which result. Throughout the period, for example, there were very good reasons why the managements were anxious to keep *total* production wages to a minimum. The economic situation described in Chapter 7 required action to keep all costs in check. If not the largest single item in total costs, production wages were one of the largest items which were subject to management control. More significantly, a number of published reports confirmed what

32. For example, one overseer was recently called before the Branch Committee for using intemperate language in a conversation with the FOC. He had asked the FOC if *he* would ask members of the chapel to remove some waste in the publishing department.

the managements knew only too well:[33] production wages were very much inflated because of over-manning. Not only did this knowledge act as a special incentive to do something about the situation, but it also made it impossible to justify increases in earnings during the Labour Government's incomes policy without engaging in some form of productivity bargaining.[34]

Negotiation of Comprehensive Agreements

It might be thought, then, that the negotiation of comprehensive agreements would be significant for the findings in Chapters 2, 3 and 4. In 1970, for example, the NBPI remarked that:

There is no doubt that the national newspaper industry is making an effort to achieve more realistic manning levels. Since our last report there has been a great deal of activity in the negotiation of productivity agreements between managements and unions which are described as comprehensive agreements. These are not 'comprehensive' in the usual sense as they are negotiated with individual chapels each representing relatively few workers. However, they do cover a wide range of work practices and conditions of employment, principally reduction in manning levels, reduction or elimination of overtime or payment for overtime and consolidation of wage rates and allowances. Invariably they provide for the sharing of cost savings between the company and the employees concerned.[35]

As the NBPI suggests, the use of the word 'comprehensive' to describe these agreements is rather odd. It also has an interesting history. The Electricians have claimed that they were the first to introduce it soon after the strike in 1955.[36] It appeared, they say, in the phrase 'an upstanding wage for a comprehensive service' which was a major policy objective of the EETPU in the 1960s. But the type of comprehensive agreement involving Electricians and Engineers came relatively late in the day. The main feature was the elimination or reduction in the overtime working which in the 1950s and 1960s had become extensive; the overtime payments were simply consolidated into a single equated weekly rate and the rotas and shifts re-organized.

33. In 1957 the NPA had set up an Efficiency of Production Committee to make productivity comparisons between 1937 and 1957. Needless to say, there were very few cases in which 1957 compared favourably with 1937.
34. Of the four grounds under which exceptional pay increases were available, the only one applicable to Fleet Street was an improvement in productivity.
35. Report No. 141, *Costs and Revenue of National Newspapers*, Cmnd. 4277 (London: HMSO, 1969), p. 14.
36. The 1955 strike is described in the notes to Chapter 8.

The more typical type of comprehensive agreement involved a reduction in the number of jobs in a department and a sharing of the savings between the management and chapel. The pattern for this type of agreement was set by an agreement in 1963 between the NPA and the LCB of SOGAT. The background is as follows. A previous agreement of 1960 had stipulated that on the introduction of mechanization into the publishing department no regular could be made redundant, and reductions in the number of jobs could only take place as a result of natural attrition. The savings from the introduction of mechanization did not come quickly enough for some managements and so they pressured the NPA to re-open negotiations. The result was the 1963 agreement which set down guide-lines to be followed by the managements and chapels in each office. The number of casual jobs, the agreement said, could be reduced by negotiation, and in return the chapel should share in the savings: the first 10% would go to the managements and the remainder would be divided 50-50 between the management and the chapel. There should also be some regularization of casual jobs. In the agreements which resulted, 'comprehensive' often came to be applied to the staffing levels.

The agreement between the *Daily Mirror* and the Machine branch of NATSOPA on the move of the newspaper to new plant at Holborn Circus similarly set the pattern for negotiations between the NPA and the branch, which were finally concluded in 1966. The agreement was very similar to that between the NPA and the London Central Branch. Negotiations were to take place between the managements and chapels about reductions in the number of jobs, the savings being shared equally. There was also to be some decasualization.

This initial impetus was taken up by the NPA under the pressure of the Labour Government's incomes policy and carried over into the industry-wide agreements which were negotiated with the printing and maintenance unions in 1968. A similar pattern was followed with guide-lines laid down for negotiations between the managements and chapels. As a result, comprehensive agreements spread their net widely, despite initial objections from the NGA. By 1970 there were very few departments which were not covered by the terms of a comprehensive agreement.

The willingness of the managements to negotiate comprehensive agreements of the variety described above needs little explanation.

Faced with the need to seek the chapels' co-operation in the introduction of new technology or the operation of new plant, the managements found that they had little alternative. As one representative explained to the Royal Commission on Trade Unions: 'It certainly is the only way at this particular moment that we have been able to find — and I think this goes for the newspapers — of initiating any form of increase in productivity without increasing the cost of production which is highly important as far as we are concerned.'[37] Once the precedent had been set, it was difficult to change, despite mounting fears about the effect of comprehensive agreements on the internal pay structures.[38] Furthermore, the prices and incomes policy of the Labour Government provided an impetus of its own as has already been pointed out.

Some managers also argue that comprehensive agreements had advantages other than reductions in the number of jobs which helped to minimize costs. For the very first time they were able to codify many existing payments and practices, in some cases introducing rudimentary cost controls. Comprehensive agreements also provided an opportunity to negotiate valuable changes in working arrangements such as improvements in shift cover.

That the managements had some success in reducing the number of jobs as a result of the negotiation of comprehensive agreements is beyond doubt. In 1970, following an investigation in five main production areas in a sample of seven newspapers during the period 1967 to 1969, the NBPI concluded: 'In the production departments investigated we found that manning levels had been reduced by an average of 5% (about 530 men in the sample), ranging from an increase of 5% in one newspaper to a reduction of 15% in another.'[39] A better idea of the number of jobs which it was possible to cut down in an office can be gained by studying the examples given by the management of IPC Newspapers to the Royal Commission on Trade Unions etc.

37. Royal Commission on Trade Unions and Employers' Associations, *Minutes of Evidence, loc. cit.*, Question 9432.
38. The NBPI (Report No. 141, *op. cit.*, p. 14), for example, warned that 'it is likely to be increasingly difficult to continue with fragmented productivity bargaining without provoking wage claims based on the need to store traditional differentials.'
39. *ibid.*, p. 13.

In 1961 the agreed night staff in the publishing department of the *Daily Mirror* was:

	20pp.	24pp.	28pp.	32pp.
	539	631	713	713
including	100 casuals	119 casuals	208 casuals	208 casuals

Negotiations in 1964 for eliminating casual labour resulted in a nightly working staff of 447, including casual labour as follows:

20pp.	24pp.	28pp.	32pp.
75	62	65	69

Since then the nightly staff has been reduced to 353 for all sizes. A 50% share of the savings has been divided among the remaining staff.

In 1961 the agreed number of assistants (SOGAT Division I) in the machine room of the *Daily Mirror* was:

	20pp.	24pp.	28pp.	32pp.
	616	643	740	744
including	210 casuals	240 casuals	260 casuals	260 casuals

Negotiations in 1964 for eliminating casual labour resulted in a nightly working staff of 541 and this figure included on average, 10 casuals. A 50% share of the savings was shared among the remaining staff.

Similar negotiations for the *Sunday Mirror* in 1964 and 1966 also resulted in staff reductions. For example, for issues of 40pp. the numbers were reduced from 852 to 602 in the machine room and from 828 to 551 in the publishing department. The savings were shared on a 50-50 basis.[40]

Evidence to suggest that the managements were able to reduce *total* production wages as a result of exercises of this kind is available in Tables 10.1 to 10.4 which compare changes in *total* production wages with changes in earnings.[41] In the periods 1961 to 1964 and 1964 to 1967 there was either a reduction in *total* production wages or an increase smaller than the increase in earnings in a number of offices: in the period 1961 to 1964 office D stands out; and in the period 1964 to 1967 offices C, D, F and H stand out. In the period 1967 to 1970, on the other hand, no office is comparable.

Yet it would be wrong to exaggerate the significance of the negotiation of comprehensive agreements. Any conclusions reached as a result of comparing the changes in *total* production wages with the changes in earnings in Tables 10.1 to 10.4 must be treated with

40. Royal Commission on Trade Unions and Employers' Associations, *Minutes of Evidence, loc. cit.*, p. 2566. See also the discussion on the NATSOPA agreement by W. Shultz and R. B. McKersie, 'Stimulating Productivity: Choices, Problems and Shares', *British Journal of Industrial Relations* (March 1967).
41. The reader is reminded that the NPA collects details of total production wages for the period 1 July to 30 June in each year. See Chapter 7.

TABLES 10.1 and 10.2
PERCENTAGE CHANGES IN TOTAL PRODUCTION WAGES

1961-64

Office	A	B	C	D	E	F	G	H	I	J
Composing/ Reading	64.0[31.7]	48.0[19.2]	38.0[30.5]	24.0[19.5]	32.0[5.6]	24.0 [23.8]	31.0[19.3]	59.0[43.1]	31.0[14.3]	32.0[33.7]
Foundry/ Process	46.0[32.0]	38.0[26.7]	37.0[25.8]	1.0[22.2]	18.0[15.1]	26.0 [15.0]	25.0 [9.7]	30.0 [16.0]	32.0[31.0]	22.0 [7.7]
Machine	49.0[17.3]	65.0[36.3]	40.0[20.6]	11.0[22.7]	27.0[9.6]	35.0 [35.6]	18.0[23.0]	54.0 [46.3]	24.0[16.5]	31.0[12.0]
Publishing	59.0[29.6]	62.0[34.5]	45.0[22.0]	1.0[24.2]	22.0[19.5]	31.0 [33.4]	29.0[19.8]	48.0 [21.2]	21.0[29.0]	29.0[10.1]

1964-67

Office	A	B	C	D	E	F	G	H	I	J
Composing/ Reading	28.0[19.6]	13.0[21.8]	0.3 [1.1]	17.0[15.0]	30.0[44.4]	4.0 [9.6]	33.0[33.5]	−2.0 [13.6]	10.0[14.5]	36.0[23.0]
Foundry/ Process	22.0[14.3]	13.0[1.7]	−6.0[−2.9]	−7.0[9.5]	13.0[5.7]	1.0 [−5.8]	0 [0.9]	8.0 [−7.7]	15.0 [2.9]	29.0[40.3]
Machine	47.0[18.0]	12.0[3.2]	−5.0[−9.3]	12.0[7.8]	15.0[16.7]	−11.0[−15.2]	0 [3.8]	−7.0[−3.8]	8.0[21.8]	164.0[49.8]
Publishing	38.0[39.2]	15.0[7.7]	−9.0[3.8]	−4.0[6.0]	12.0[21.3]	4.0 [14.3]	13.0[11.3]	−7.0 [8.1]	11.0[17.0]	85.0[32.0]

Note: The changes in earnings of a *representative* occupation are shown in brackets.

TABLES 10.3 and 10.4

PERCENTAGE CHANGES IN UNIT PRODUCTION WAGES

1967-70

Office	A	B	C	D	E	F	G	H	I	J
Composing/Reading	68.0 [51.9]	38.0 [42.2]	41.0[46.1]	64.0 [47.7]	57.0 [55.8]	29.0[42.2]	42.0 [34.3]	0 [39.1]	20.0[28.4]	25.0 [35.0]
Foundry/Process	34.0 [33.7]	17.0 [28.5]	26.0[29.7]	24.0 [15.0]	43.0 [64.2]	7.0 [22.8]	20.0 [25.4]	22.0 [31.1]	13.0[22.2]	6.0 [36.4]
Machine	64.0 [64.3]	39.0 [39.7]	32.0[21.7]	26.0 [42.2]	39.0 [41.2]	38.0[45.4]	21.0.[31.3]	33.0[57.9]	11.0[11.6]	16.0 [6.3]
Publishing	27.0 [38.5]	25.0 [18.4]	21.0[30.1]	39.0 [28.3]	41.0 [42.4]	11.0[16.8]	15.0 [16.8]	10.0 [60.5]	12.0[11.7]	36.0 [44.0]

1961-70

Office	A	B	C	D	E	F	G	H	I	J
Composing/Reading	254.0[139.2]	131.0[107.1]	94.0[67.3]	139.0[102.9]	168.0[137.4]	65.0[93.1]	148.0[114.0]	150.0[126.1]	72.0[68.0]	122.5[122.3]
Foundry/Process	139.0[101.1]	82.0[60.9]	63.0[34.0]	17.0[53.9]	91.0[99.8]	36.0[33.0]	50.0[38.6]	57.0[40.4]	73.0[64.8]	67.8[94.7]
Machine	261.0[139.6]	157.0[96.6]	75.0[33.2]	56.0[71.1]	103.0[79.8]	66.0[67.2]	42.0[67.5]	92.0[122.2]	50.0[47.8]	302.0[78.3]
Publishing	180.0[165.3]	133.0[83.4]	59.0[61.8]	36.0[86.3]	92.0[106.3]	51.0[88.2]	67.0[55.7]	50.0[110.3]	51.0[53.4]	224.0[130.2]

Note: The changes in earnings of a *representative* occupation are shown in brackets.

the utmost caution in view of the inadequacy of the data, but, contrary to expectation, the offices which were able to achieve a reduction in *total* production wages (or an increase smaller than the increase in earnings) were not the offices with the above-average increases in earnings. Office D is the prime example. Moreover, the departments in which the reductions took place, 'Foundry/Process', 'Machine', and 'Publishing', were not the departments with the above-average increases in earnings. The opposite is true: the departments with the above-average increases in earnings, 'Composing/Reading', were also the departments with the above-average increases in *total* production wages.

Advantages of Payment by Task

In practice, the simplest method of establishing the influence of the managements is to examine more closely the findings in Chapter 8. For example, it was argued there that the large number and variety of components of pay could be explained if it was accepted that the chapels have used the payment system to control the impact of discontinuities in production on working arrangements. But, to be complete, this argument needs to take into account the advantages to the managements of what has become, in effect, a system of payment by task. Because of the many changes in the product and fluctuations in the level of activity in the product market, the over-riding need is to keep *unit* production wages to a minimum. Since the managements are unable to adjust to changes in the demand for labour in the usual way, a system of payment by task has one obvious advantage: it ensures that a payment is only made when the task is performed.[42] In the case of the extras which are negotiated by the NPA and the trade unions it also ensures that they do not multiply the other components of pay when the industry basic rates are increased.

Some of the other findings in previous chapters now begin to fall into place. The differences and changes in earnings by office, which Chapter 7 has established were associated with differences and changes in page sizes, no longer pose a problem. The result of a system of payment by task is that those offices which make the most changes and have the most fluctuations will also have the largest

42. In other words, there is an alteration in the labour supply curve.

increase in earnings. To quote again the example in Chapter 8, if Permanent Time Hands in two offices receive four hours' overtime for each 48pp. issue, then it stands to reason that earnings will be higher in the office which runs more 48pp. issues. The same argument can be used to explain differences in the three periods which Chapter 7 established were associated with changes in page sizes. The period 1964 to 1967 witnessed a reduction in page sizes in a number of offices due to the economic depression which led up to and followed devaluation. Finally, the argument also helps to explain why the newspaper which was making substantial profits during the period was not among the highest paying offices or those with above-average increases in earnings.

To put the argument to a further test, changes in *unit* production wages were compared with changes in earnings.[43] The results are shown in Tables 10.5 to 10.8. It is significant that in each of the three periods a number of offices were able to achieve a reduction in *unit* production wages or an increase smaller than the increase in earnings; indeed, over the period 1961 to 1970 only offices C and F were unable to do this. It is also significant that the offices which were able to achieve the largest reductions in *unit* production wages were also the offices with the above-average increase in earnings.[44] Offices A, B, H and J come into this category. Offices C and F, on the other hand, had above-average increases in *unit* production wages and below-average increases in earnings. So it would appear that those offices with above-average increases in page sizes also

43. *Unit* production wages were calculated as follows. In the case of 'Composing/Reading' and 'Foundry/Process' total production wages for the period 1 July to 30 June were divided by the number of pages, i.e. average size x the number of issues. If a newspaper was also printed in Manchester, it was assumed that none of the pages used in London was produced in Manchester or, if they were, that they represented the same proportion from one year to the next. In the case of 'Machine' and 'Publishing' total production wages were divided by total pagination, i.e. copy sales x average page size x the number of issues. If a newspaper was also printed in Manchester, total production wages in London and Manchester have been combined. The figures shown later in this section are £ per page in the case of 'Composing/Reading' and 'Foundry/Process' and £ per 1,000 pages in the case of 'Machine' and 'Publishing'. For details of the different variables, see notes 2, 5 and 8 in Chapter 7.

44. There was also some evidence to suggest that the offices with the highest earnings had the lowest *unit* production wages and vice versa. However, the picture which emerged was complicated by the difference of emphasis placed by quality and popular newspapers on 'first copy' and mass production costs and by the special circumstances of the evening newspapers whose edition deadlines are much tighter.

TABLES 10.5 and 10.6
PERCENTAGE CHANGES IN UNIT PRODUCTION WAGES

1961-64

Office	A	B	C	D	E	F	G	H	I	J
Composing/Reading	35.3[31.7]	24.5[19.2]	24.7[30.5]	11.7[19.5]	16.0[5.6]	11.8 [23.8]	15.1[19.3]	35.0[43.1]	7.0[14.3]	31.1[33.7]
Foundry/Process	19.5[32.0]	15.6[26.7]	24.2[25.8]	−8.9[22.2]	2.6[15.1]	14.2 [15.0]	10.1[9.7]	11.5[16.0]	12.2[31.0]	21.9[1.7]
Machine	8.6[17.3]	27.8[36.3]	35.3[20.6]	−6.8[22.7]	18.5[9.6]	30.2 [35.6]	12.5[23.0]	−5.3[46.3]	19.7[16.5]	30.9[12.0]
Publishing	15.6[37.6]	28.9[43.9]	36.2[19.8]	−13.1[37.0]	14.4[19.5]	27.6 [33.4]	23.0[19.8]	−4.5[21.2]	16.6[29.0]	29.0[10.1]

1964-67

Office	A	B	C	D	E	F	G	H	I	J
Composing/Reading	9.4[19.6]	10.8[21.8]	16.3 [1.1]	18.6[15.0]	—	20.6 [9.6]	—	8.9 [13.6]	10.2[14.5]	3.9[23.0]
Foundry/Process	4.6[14.3]	11.4 [1.7]	9.0[−2.9]	−5.2 [9.5]	—	17.2 [−5.8]	—	8.7[−7.7]	15.7 [2.9]	−0.5[40.3]
Machine	23.0[18.0]	3.5 [3.2]	16.7[−9.3]	12.1 [7.8]	—	14.8[−15.2]	—	−0.5[−3.8]	5.2[21.8]	34.9[49.8]
Publishing	15.7[39.2]	39.0 [7.7]	12.3 [3.8]	−1.4 [6.0]	—	27.9 [14.3]	—	3.7 [8.1]	8.1[17.0]	−5.1 [32.0]

Note: The changes in earnings of a *representative* occupation are shown in brackets.

TABLES 10.7 and 10.8
PERCENTAGE CHANGES IN UNIT PRODUCTION WAGES

1967-70

Office	A	B	C	D	E	F	G	H	I	J
Composing/Reading	43.1[31.7]	37.9[19.2]	37.5[30.5]	62.6[19.5]	—	23.1[42.2]	—	30.4[39.1]	10.5[28.4]	23.4[35.0]
Foundry/Process	13.8[33.7]	16.6[28.5]	23.3[29.1]	22.2[15.0]	—	2.1[22.8]	—	−0.7[31.1]	4.3[22.2]	4.6[36.4]
Machine	27.5[64.3]	33.2[39.7]	44.6[21.7]	43.8[42.2]	—	48.3[45.4]	—	−9.3[33.0]	21.0[11.6]	23.1[6.3]
Publishing	−1.3[38.5]	22.0[18.4]	34.0[30.1]	55.8[28.3]	—	27.4[16.8]	—	22.0[60.5]	22.0[11.7]	43.7[44.0]

1961-70

Office	A	B	C	D	E	F	G	H	I	J
Composing/Reading	111.8[139.2]	90.1[107.1]	99.4[67.3]	115.4[102.9]	—	66.0[93.1]	—	91.6[126.1]	30.3[68.0]	68.1[122.3]
Foundry/Process	42.3[101.7]	50.2[60.9]	66.8[34.0]	5.5[53.9]	—	36.7[33.0]	—	20.4[40.4]	35.5[64.8]	26.9[94.7]
Machine	70.4[139.6]	76.2[96.6]	128.4[33.2]	50.3[77.1]	—	121.7[67.2]	—	−14.6[122.2]	52.5[47.8]	117.3[78.3]
Publishing	31.9[165.3]	69.6[83.4]	105.0[61.8]	33.5[86.3]	—	108.0[88.2]	—	−22.7[110.3]	53.7[53.4]	75.1[130.2]

Note: The changes in earnings of a *representative* occupation are shown in brackets.

enjoyed some of the advantages of the economies of scale, while those with below-average increases in page sizes suffered from a kind of 'ratchet effect'.

However, there is still one puzzle which has to be explained. As in the case of *total* production wages, Tables 10.5 to 10.8 show that the departments with the reductions in *unit* production wages are not the departments with the above-average increases in earnings. But for the moment this must wait.

Significance of Comparability

It was also argued in Chapter 8 that both the similarities among the offices and the narrowing in differentials within the offices could be explained in terms of the use of comparisons by the chapels. But, to be complete, this argument too needs to take into account the significance of comparability for the managements. To take first the intensification of the use of comparisons within the offices, it is clear that the managements had little choice in the matter. The occupations which enjoyed above-average increases in earnings were patently dissatisfied with their position in the internal pay structures. More to the point, they were prepared to back up their arguments with force — something which the maintenance chapels, in particular, did on a number of occasions. The managements, then, were forced to give more attention to the internal pay structures. As Douty has argued:

The fact should be emphasised that, in many cases, management has an interest in the simplification and rationalisation of wage structures that tends broadly to parallel the trade union interest. As enterprises increase in size, as the job structure becomes more complex, and as labor force recruitment becomes a function of central personnel offices, the need for consistent and 'defensible' wage rate structures becomes apparent. Trade union pressures to correct 'inequities' in wage structures undoubtedly have contributed powerfully in many instances to management concern with the problem, and have stimulated the growth of formal procedures for the establishment and administration of wage rate structures.[45]

The fact that no office was able to achieve a reduction in *total* production wages in the period 1967 to 1970 is not without significance for the argument. Chapter 8 has already suggested that

45. H. M. Douty, 'The Impact of Trade Unionism on Internal Wage Structures', in J. L. Meij (ed.), *Internal Wage-Structure* (Amsterdam: North Holland, 1963), p. 226.

153

one reason for this was the opposition of the chapels to further reductions in the number of jobs. But equally important was the fear of disturbing differentials in the internal pay structures. The dispute described in Appendix I was a powerful reminder of what could happen as a result of negotiating comprehensive agreements chapel by chapel. Indeed, it would appear from Tables 10.1 to 10.4 and 10.5 to 10.8 that in a number of offices the managements had to use the savings which they had achieved in some departments to remedy anomalies in others. This seems to be the logical explanation for the finding that those departments with the reduction in *total* and *unit* production wages were not the departments with the above-average increases in earnings.

Turning now to the use of comparisons among the offices, Chapter 8 quoted one of the managements as saying that they had no choice but to accept the comparisons which the chapels made with other offices. But this totally underestimates the part played by managers in the process. Not only do they accept the legitimacy of comparisons which are made with other offices, the industrial relations managers very often take the initiative in the search for them. As the next chapter will show, they also used membership of the NPA for this purpose. The reason is quite simple. In the negotiating process these comparisons have one inestimable advantage: they offer solutions to problems which would otherwise involve a straightforward power struggle. As Ross has put it in a now much-quoted section:

The ready-made settlement supplies an answer, a solution, a formula. It is mutually face-saving . . . it is the one settlement which permits both parties to believe they have done a proper job, the one settlement which has the best chance of being 'sold' to the company's board of directors and the union's rank and file. [46]

But the use of comparisons between offices has even greater importance than this in the longer term. By extending components of pay and other practices from one office to another, this 'parity' or 'pattern' bargaining helped to equalize *unit* production wages and so take them out of competition.[47] Tables 10.9 to 10.12, which

46. A. M. Ross, *Trade Union Wage Policy* (Berkeley: University of California Press, 1948), p. 52.
47. For a discussion of 'pattern bargaining' in the USA, see H. M. Levinson, 'Pattern Bargaining: a case study of the Automobile Workers', *Quarterly Journal of Economics* (May 1960); M. Reder, 'The Theory of Union Wage Policy', *The Review of Economics and Statistics* (Feb. 1952); G. Seltzer, 'Pattern Bargaining and the United Steelworkers', *Journal of Political Economy* (Aug.

give details of the spread of the *unit* production wages of eight of the offices, go some way towards showing this. The spread of *unit* production wages was largest in 'Foundry/Process', the smallest cost centre. (There are also special considerations in this case which cannot be discussed without revealing the identity of some of the newspapers.) In the other departments the spread is much smaller. In 'Composing/Reading' the fact that the spread of *unit* production wages was larger than the spread of earnings is hardly surprising in view of the differences between the 'first copy' of the newspapers. In 'Publishing' the spread of *unit* production wages was only slightly larger than the spread of earnings. The most significant result is to be found in 'Machine', the largest cost centre in most of the offices. Here the spread of *unit* production wages was smaller than the spread of earnings; in three of the four years both the ranges and the coefficients of variation were less.

The results were even more remarkable when the *unit* production wages of newspapers within the same categories were compared with one another. In 1961, for example, the *unit* production wages in 'Machine' of the two evening newspapers were exactly the same — £152.2! In 1964 they were still very close — £171.3 and £180.4. In 1961 in 'Composing/Reading' of the same newspapers they were £81.4 and £81.0; in 1964 they were £93.7 and £94.0. In 1961 in 'Publishing' they were £139.2 and £140.4; in 1964 they were £171.2 and £160.6. There were also similarities among the quality and popular newspapers. In 1964 the *unit* production wages in 'Machine' of two quality newspapers were £82.7 and £84.3; in 1967 they were £92.7 and £98.4. In 1970 in 'Composing/Reading' of two quality newspapers they were £104.9 and £106.3. In 1970 in 'Machine' of two quality newspapers they were £121.1 and £127.0.

So the attitudes and policies of the managements were not without significance for the findings in Chapters 2, 3 and 4. The system of payment by task, which Chapter 8 suggested is the key to

---

1951). Most of these studies present evidence to suggest that trade unions are prepared to allow firms to break the 'pattern' in order to keep them going. The fact that this seems to have happened in Fleet Street so rarely can be explained by the system of payment by task. The newspaper which is losing circulation or advertising receives some compensation because payments and manning levels also tend to reduce. This, again, emphasizes that *unit* production wages are the key.

TABLE 10.9
INTER-OFFICE UNIT PRODUCTION WAGES: 1961

	Range: Lowest to Highest %	Coefficient of Variation %
Composing/Reading	176.7	27.1
Foundry/Process	554.9	59.5
Machine	116.5	28.5
Publishing	228.8	36.3

TABLE 10.10
INTER-OFFICE UNIT PRODUCTION WAGES: 1964

	Range: Lowest to Highest %	Coefficient of Variation %
Composing/Reading	155.6	24.4
Foundry/Process	523.0	54.0
Machine	54.4	18.7
Publishing	155.5	33.4

TABLE 10.11
INTER-OFFICE UNIT PRODUCTION WAGES: 1967

	Range: Lowest to Highest %	Coefficient of Variation %
Composing/Reading	146.3	25.0
Foundry/Process	366.4	53.0
Machine	59.0	16.8
Publishing	118.3	29.9

TABLE 10.12
INTER-OFFICE UNIT PRODUCTION WAGES: 1970

	Range: Lowest to Highest %	Coefficient of Variation %
Composing/Reading	188.0	31.2
Foundry/Process	474.3	56.5
Machine	63.1	14.4
Publishing	100.2	23.7

understanding not only the large number and variety of components of pay but also the differences and changes in earnings, helps to keep *unit* production wages to a minimum. Similarly, the 'parity' or 'pattern' bargaining which helps to explain the similarities between the offices also has advantages for the managements. Not only does it provide solutions to problems which would otherwise involve a straightforward power struggle, it also helps to take *unit* production wages out of competition. It only remains now to examine the role of the employers' association.

Chapter 11

The Employers' Association

The Newspaper Publishers Association is the employers' association of the national newspapers printed in London and Manchester.[1] It is not to be confused with the Newspaper Society which is the employers' association of the provincial morning, evening and weekly newspapers in England and Wales, and weekly newspapers in the London area. There are also two employers' associations in Scotland. The employers' association of the daily and evening newspapers is known as the Scottish Daily Newspaper Society and the association of the weekly newspapers as the Scottish Newspaper Proprietors' Association.

A committee set up in 1968 under the chairmanship of Sir William Haley to investigate the activities of the NPA reported that it should act in any area in which national newspapers shared a common interest and in which it was realistic to organize activities collectively. Industrial relations, therefore, is not the only activity of the NPA. It is involved in many of the activities of a trade association, including advertising, distribution, newsprint and press facilities;[2] in fact, throughout the period with which this study is concerned the NPA was registered as a limited company and not as a trade union.

The governing body of the NPA is the Council. The 1947 articles

1. The NPA was formed in 1906 as a result of the decision of a number of newspaper proprietors to withdraw from the LMPA. There was a dispute at the London printing firm of Hamptons during which the LSC threatened strike action against all members of the association. The newspaper proprietors agreed to make separate agreements with the LSC on condition that it did not involve the newspapers in the disputes in the printing industry.
2. For example, the NPA negotiates with British Rail for the carriage of newspapers, vets advertising agencies and advertisements and organizes press facilities. The NPA decided to register under the Industrial Relations Act in respect of its industrial relations activities.

of association provided that each member newspaper should have a representative, who is usually the proprietor, together with two alternates who are entitled to attend Council meetings and to speak on the representative's behalf. The officers of the Council are a Chairman and Vice-Chairman who are chosen by the representatives, usually from among their number. Sir William Haley's committee also recommended the setting up of an Executive Committee which could deal with the increase in the number and complexity of the NPA's activities. The Executive Committee, which now meets regularly each month, is composed of the managing directors of the major companies, and its officers are the Chairman and Vice-Chairman of the Council.

In 1959 the Labour Committee, which previously had negotiated with the trade unions and advised the Council on industrial relations matters, was replaced by the Labour Executive. It was intended to be more than a change of name. Much of the thinking behind the setting up of the new committee is to be found in a memorandum written by the then Labour Secretary in January of that year, in which he pointed to the weaknesses of the NPA's handling of industrial relations. The Labour Committee, he argued, was constantly under pressure. 'The Labour Committee only had time to consider the unions' claims.' The 'initiative', he added, 'always lies with the unions', resulting in the piecemeal addition of agreements to the main 1947 agreements.[3] The NPA, he concluded, must seek to take the initiative despite the constraints imposed by the weakness of the managements' bargaining position.

The intention was that the Labour Executive, which was to be composed of a small number of managing directors and general managers, men of standing hand-picked by the Council and able to commit the industry to an agreed course of action, should set a completely new pattern in industrial relations in Fleet Street. The members of the Executive tried but failed. The proprietors have not been prepared to give them the necessary authority, the Council intervening more and more in negotiations with the trade unions in order to protect their individual, and very often conflicting, interests. For reasons that will emerge in the final chapter, these interests also help to explain the lack of motivation to make changes.

A second committee which merits attention is the London Labour

3. The agreements negotiated in 1947 form the foundation for those which followed. The basic outline has changed very little.

Committee. Established at the same time as the Labour Executive, it is composed of the industrial relations managers from each of the offices. The intention was that this committee should advise the Labour Executive on matters of detail. Over the years, however, it has taken on the additional responsibilities of negotiating with individual branches and the surveillance of the House Claims procedure which is discussed in the second section of this chapter.

The number of full-time officials employed by the NPA has increased considerably in recent years, largely as a result of the increase in the number of the association's activities. By 1970 there were three industrial relations advisers as well as the Director who has special responsibility for industrial relations. The Advisors service the two labour committees, and at different times during the period also acted as chief negotiators. The greater part of their time, however, is taken up in providing an advisory service to members of the London Labour Committee on domestic problems, often becoming involved with the full-time trade union officers during disputes.

The reasons for giving separate attention to the NPA are the same as in the case of the trade unions. First, the NPA is responsible for negotiating revisions to the industry basic rates. It is important to find out why there were no major changes in the structure of these rates, despite the disputes in 1968 and 1970, and despite the setting up of the Joint Board for the National Newspaper Industry[4] and the National Newspaper Steering Group.[5] Secondly, the NPA may seek to influence the outcome of negotiations between the managements and chapels, and it is important to know what form this takes and what effect, if any, this had.

4. The Joint Board for the National Newspaper Industry was set up under the independent chairmanship of Lord Devlin in 1964, comprising the managing directors of the newspapers and the general secretaries of the trade unions. The intention was that the Board, whose creation the Report of the Royal Commission on the Press, 1961-2, had recommended, should undertake the reform of industrial relations in Fleet Street. Unfortunately the Board was unable to make real progress, the main stumbling block being the problem of deciding how savings from improvements in productivity should be shared among the members of the trade unions. By 1967 the unions were more concerned to negotiate revisions to the industry basic rates, and the Board gradually passed into history. The one legacy of the Board was the EIU Report which had been commissioned in its early days.

5. The National Newspaper Steering Group was an attempt to revive the Joint Board, this time without an independent chairman. It followed the *Daily Mirror* Machine Managers' dispute in 1969 and the SOGAT dispute in 1970, both of

The Employers' Association and the Industry Basic Rates

The very absence of major changes in their structure is the most significant finding of this study so far as the industry basic rates are concerned. It is also surprising. The subject of the pay structure figured prominently in discussions between the NPA and the trade unions, especially during the latter part of the period. On a number of occasions the NPA had no choice but to negotiate with the unions separately, and some took the opportunity to press for improvements in their members' relative position or to alter the terms already agreed with other unions.

The members of the NPA themselves were not dissatisfied with the structure of the industry basic rates. The NPA, in fact, only included the subject on the agenda of discussions with the unions for two reasons. First, improvements in pay seemed to be the only way of involving the unions in discussions about increasing efficiency of production — a major objective. Secondly, negotiations between the management and chapels began to lead to dissatisfaction with the internal pay structures, the disputes described in Appendix I being an excellent example. It seemed that the only way to remedy this problem was to discuss the matter collectively with the unions.

But it proved impossible for the NPA to formulate clear-cut proposals on the pay structure. There was little common ground between the managements. There were also too many uncertainties involved. In both the instances quoted above, it was difficult to spell out proposals in advance of discussions with the unions. The NPA, for example, could not say how the savings from increased efficiency in production would be used until it had some idea of their size. It could not say what the differentials should be in the new pay structure until it had sounded out the reactions of the unions. It could not do either of these because of the union's inability to co-operate with one another; sometimes it could not hold joint meetings because one or other of the unions refused to attend. This

which had confirmed fears about the effects of fragmented bargaining. The Steering Group, however, was short-lived. The climate was changing rapidly. The trade unions were primarily concerned with the unemployment in the printing industry, worsened by the forthcoming closure of the *Daily Sketch*; so it was not possible for them to talk about reductions in the number of jobs. The managements had their own problems and Rupert Murdoch's takeover of the *Sun* from IPC Newspapers Ltd had intensified the competition between the newspapers.

explains why the NPA took the initiative in setting up the Joint Board for the National Newspaper Industry and the National Newspaper Steering Group. It was anxious to establish a permanent industry body, representative of the managements and the unions, to which industrial relations problems could be referred for solutions binding on all the parties.

But, ironically, the NPA's weakness was also its strength. There is one very simple explanation for the disputes in 1968, 1970 and 1971: the NPA cannot treat one union more favourably than the others unless they give at least their tacit consent. The NPA's philosophy is summed up in the report of the Court of Inquiry investigating the strike of Engineers and Electricians in 1955:

> It could not do otherwise than treat the revisions of wage settlements as a comprehensive job and that on this occasion the customary practice had been followed. It was a basic principle of these wage discussions that no union was granted preferential treatment over any other union and that in practice all the unions took and expected to receive their customary differentials.[6]

Influence on Negotiations between Managements and Chapels

Like the trade unions, the NPA inevitably has some influence on negotiations between the managements and chapels through the industry agreements. As Chapter 9 has already pointed out, the most significant example in this period was the various agreements which laid down the guide-lines for the negotiation of comprehensive agreements. But it remains to be seen if the NPA was able to influence the outcome of these negotiations and what effect, if any, this had.

In fact, a systematic attempt to influence the outcome of these negotiations began in 1961 following a series of claims submitted by SLADE chapels. The Council agreed that no management should settle further claims involving SLADE members without first informing the newly formed Labour Executive. This arrangement was placed on a more formal footing in December 1964, following the revisions to the industry basic rates, and it was extended to all unions. In the event of a claim the managements were required to submit to the NPA a standard *pro forma* giving details of the chapel, the date of the claim, and the substance of the claim. The claims

6. *Report of a Court of Inquiry into a dispute between members of the NPA and members of the AEU and ETU*, Cmnd. 9439 (London: HMSO, 1955), pp. 7-8.

were then considered by the London Labour Committee at their regular Friday meeting, and the appropriate advice given.

One of the reasons for introducing what became known as the House Claims procedure was the NPA's concern at the negotiation of additional payments during periods of wage stabilization. But this was not the only reason. The following statement, contained in a letter from the NPA (8 December 1964) to the managements, set out some of the thinking behind the introduction of the procedure:

The NPA Council decided . . . to impose an obligation on all offices to report to the NPA all house claims which, if met, would result in additional payments or a reduction in working hours. This would provide the opportunity for collective discussion of the claims with particular reference to possible repercussive effects.

It was argued that a pooling of knowledge and experience would be beneficial; arguments which had been used successfully to reject a claim in one office might be used in other offices. At the very least, its supporters argued, the procedure would ensure that the managements were in full possession of the facts, making it less likely that they would concede claims based on half-truths. There was one final reason for introducing the procedure. If a dispute occurred as a result of the rejection of a claim, the other managements would inevitably become involved; it was important, therefore, that they should be aware of the circumstances leading up to the dispute and be in a position to offer advice.

The NPA kept detailed records of the claims submitted under the House Claims procedure for the first year of its operation, showing that 107 claims were reported. After the first year, the scope of negotiations between the management and chapels began to change: the number of straightforward claims began to decline, and were replaced by negotiations on comprehensive agreements. To meet this development, the members of the London Labour Committee agreed to inform the committee as soon as these negotiations began; to keep the NPA officials informed of any major developments; and to submit to the committee a draft of the final proposals before they were agreed with the chapel.

It is difficult to evaluate the effectiveness of the House Claims procedure. Patently it failed to put a stop to drift, but with the managements themselves often eager to negotiate with the chapels, this was to be expected. There were examples of managements failing to report claims or agreements, but this was not a major weakness. More significant were the problems inherent in the

163

negotiating process itself. In practice, the guide-lines which the members of the London Labour Committee had set themselves proved to be unworkable; industrial relations managers found that they often had to commit themselves step by step in negotiations with the chapels about comprehensive agreements, and were able to report only the final agreement to the committee. Without the right of veto, some members argued, the London Labour Committee was powerless to undo what the majority believed to be most damaging to their interests; they pointed out that many significant concessions had been made in this way. But this argument missed the point. Very often the management which had made the concession had done so as a result of the threat of industrial action by the chapel. Unless the NPA could offer more than its moral support, the exercise of a veto would have been an empty gesture.

However, it would be wrong to infer from this that the NPA had no influence. The House Claims procedure was extremely significant, since it legitimized the use of comparisons by providing the industrial relations managers with an opportunity to discuss and exchange information about the situation in the different offices. This helps to explain the similarities between the internal pay structures.

Chapter 12

Summary and Conclusions

If nothing else, this study has shown that there is no single explanation for the pay structure in Fleet Street. As in other industries, the pay structure in the production and maintenance departments of the newspaper offices is an extremely complex phenomenon; the attitudes and policies of the parties which shape it are influenced by a multitude of different factors. But at the risk of over-simplifying what has been a complicated argument, there would seem to be one conclusion which stands out: the key to understanding the main features of the pay structure as well as many of the other characteristics which have come to be associated with industrial relations in Fleet Street is what might be termed the 'sub-contracting' relationship between the managements and chapels.

The term 'sub-contracting' is used advisedly. Enough has been said in previous chapters to confirm that the managements exercise little or no executive control in the production and maintenance departments in Fleet Street. The first-line managers who are most closely involved with the chapels are not in practice responsible for man-management in their departments. In effect theirs is a technical role only. Put simply, the industrial relations manager manages by negotiation or, more specifically, through the payment system. The chapels, for their part, undertake to perform a number of tasks in the manufacturing process. As the preamble to one typical comprehensive agreement states: 'The purpose of this agreement, which covers hours, payments and working arrangements, is to provide a comprehensive production service.' To all intents and purposes, the chapels have a relatively free hand in making decisions about working arrangements; to quote Sykes, they are 'self-governing' associations.[1] In many departments it is the

1.   A. J. M. Sykes, 'Trade Union Workshop Organisation in the Printing Industry

165

FOC or other chapel officers who hire the workers, allocate them to the different tasks, discipline them, draw up the overtime and holiday rotas — and all this with the authority of the workers themselves.

How and why did this 'sub-contracting' relationship develop? In Fleet Street changes in the product and fluctuations in the level of activity occur so often that the chapels have been obliged to seek some control over the discontinuities in production which result. Yet these changes and fluctuations also provide the chapels with the opportunity to do this simply and effectively by forcing the managements to secure their co-operation. The result is a system of payment by task which helps to explain not only the large number and variety of components of pay but also the differences and changes in earnings. But this struggle over the supply of effort also extends to a struggle over the demand and supply of labour. In the machine and publishing departments in particular the chapels have been obliged to seek a similar form of control in order to protect themselves against the worst abuses of casual employment. Consequently, the number of jobs has become as much a part of the negotiating process as the components of pay. [2]

The struggles mentioned above were especially intense in the period immediately following the end of newsprint rationing in 1956. A stable situation in which page sizes had been restricted by government orders was followed by one in which newspapers vied with each other to increase page sizes in order to gain the maximum advantage from their monopoly of advertising. As Associated Newspapers Ltd explained in their written evidence to the Royal Commission on the Press, 1961-2:

Reviewing the experience of the last twenty years it can be stated that in the immediate post-war years during which rationing of sizes was still severe, staffs were increased because of the statutory obligations to re-engage previous employees returning from the forces.

As a generalisation it can be stated that there was a surplus of printing union labour during these years and great pressure was used to improve working conditions compared with pre-war standards so as to absorb the surplus.

This was followed by a period during which the rationing of newsprint was eased by stages permitting sizes of newspapers and circulations to be increased and in consequence competition between national newspapers was intensified and

---

— The Chapel', *Human Relations* (Feb. 1960), p. 53.
2.   But it cannot be emphasized too much that the pressure on jobs comes as much, if not more, from those outside Fleet Street as those within. See the argument in Chapters 6 and 8.

managements were reluctant to risk interferences with production by resisting demands for improved pay and increased staff at each stage of the recovery to pre-war sizes of publications.[3]

But it would be wrong to infer from this that the relationship between the managements and the chapels is simply 'effort bargaining'. It is important to realize that extra effort is no longer necessarily required in order to justify negotiations taking place. For the re-opening of the contract is now as significant in this process as the substantive issue on which the negotiations take place. In short, negotiations take place whenever the management wishes to alter the contract by requiring some change in working arrangements. As has been written of a similar situation in the Durham coal-field:

the basic concept is the price agreement — a price formally negotiated between management and men for a specified amount of work in a task of defined scope — within a range of conditions accepted as applying. As soon as these boundaries are transcended the question of a new price arises and fresh negotiations begin.[4]

It might be thought that the negotiation of comprehensive agreements would have made a difference, but this is not so. Most comprehensive agreements are quite explicit on this point; to quote a typical example, again: 'Nothing in this agreement precludes Management or Chapel from initiating negotiations to amend the Agreement as a result of changing circumstances.'

It must be obvious that the control which the chapels have been able to establish over the payment system and the demand and supply of labour goes some of the way towards explaining the high pay and over-manning in Fleet Street. But it is not only the motivation which is important. The negotiating process itself deserves some comment. The frequency of negotiations is especially significant. In the case of pay, for example, each set of negotiations introduces a new payment or level of earnings which then forms the starting-point for future negotiations. The 'haggling' which is an intrinsic part of the negotiating process is significant too. One management explained to the Royal Commission on the Press, 1961-2, how this helped to inflate the number of jobs.

3. Royal Commission on the Press, *Documentary Evidence*, Cmnd. 1812-4 (London: HMSO, 1962), p. 3. It has been argued that the problem goes back further than this to the circulation war of the 1930s. It is also argued that then and in the 1950s some proprietors were guilty of deliberately starting a 'wages race' in order to embarrass their competitors.
4. E. L. Trist *et al.*, *Organisational Choice* (London: Tavistock Publications, 1963), pp. 64-5.

These negotiations were not carried on as a scientific investigation as to the optimum number of men to be employed, but as a form of collective bargaining between the management and the chapels. Each side put forward the number of men whom they considered necessary and there was usually a wide divergence. As the result of negotiation the final figure was agreed at some mid-way point between the two proposals. The outcome of this procedure meant that the management frequently had to concede additional men whom they did not consider necessary.[5]

But there is another side to the control which the chapels have been able to establish. To all intents and purposes, they have been free to determine the unit as well as the scope of negotiations. Predictably, they have chosen the smallest unit which has the power to protect the members' interests, which in practice means the occupation or occupational grouping. The result is that negotiations with the managements are fragmented and, in extreme cases, the bargaining unit is different from the task unit. Rivalry between the chapels is intense, so that disputes like the one described in Appendix I are likely to occur at any time. It is hardly surprising, then, that the consolidation of the components of pay into single 'comprehensive' or 'equated' weekly rates had such a dramatic impact on the internal pay structures in the second half of the period.[6]

So far this chapter has given scarcely any indication of the part played by the managements in these developments. A simple answer is that they have had little choice in the matter or, in the words of one proprietor, they have 'silently given way'[7] because the chapels have had the power to impose their demands. But this answer is too simple. It does not explain why the managements have not opposed these developments with greater vigour nor does it adequately explain why so many attempts to change the situation from within have come to grief, despite the genuine intentions of the individuals involved.

The truth is that these developments have not been without advantages for the managements. It is self-evident that the control

5. Royal Commission on the Press, *op. cit.*, p. 148.
6. But the irony is that the autonomy of which the chapels are so jealous is becoming a myth so far as the negotiations of pay is concerned. The individual managements, like the NPA in its relationships with the trade unions, are quite simply unable to negotiate with one chapel without taking into account the possible reaction of the others. Had they enjoyed fewer of the trappings of power, then the chapels might have developed the joint negotiating bodies which are a feature of other industries. It remains to be seen if they can still do so.
7. David Astor, the *Observer*, 26 September 1971.

which has been conceded to the chapels is not absolutely essential to the running of the newspapers. In fact, the different groups of managers are able to devote their total energy and attention to satisfying their goals and constraints in the product market. The dominance of the proprietors is especially significant in this context. The EIU Report, for example, remarked that in some cases the proprietor had directed his energies 'solely towards the editorial function'[8] and had neglected the other aspects of the business. The chapels too are kept relatively satisfied — and because of this, it may be argued, do not make more serious demands on the managements about such matters as editorial policy.

But even these advantages are not sufficient to explain the inertia of the managements in Fleet Street. There must be other reasons why they have not opposed the developments described above more vigorously. The fact is that in a situation of rapid change a system of payment by task has obvious attractions: it ensures that a payment is made only when a given task is performed. Similarly, a system of casual employment in the machine and publishing departments ensures that labour is employed only when it is required by the work-load.

Even so, it might still be thought that the managements would be concerned lest their production wages became inflated. But this ignores the significance of the comparisons which are made between the offices. The 'parity' or 'pattern' bargaining which takes place in Fleet Street has two advantages. First, it helps the industrial relations managers to minimize conflict by providing legitimate solutions to issues which would otherwise involve a straightforward power struggle. Secondly, and more significantly in the longer term, it helps to take *unit* production wages out of competition — an advantage which, allied to the fact that profitability is not the sole or primary goal, must be regarded as the most important single reason for the inertia.

It might be thought that 'collusion' was too strong a word to describe the relationship between the managements and the chapels in Fleet Street. After all, the processes described above are much more complicated than a straightforward economic interpretation would suggest, and the consequences are for the most part unintended. Yet it is impossible to escape the conclusion that the

8. p. 52.

arrangements developed by the managements and the chapels in the light of the constraints imposed by the product market have a number of *mutual* advantages. First of all, the concentration of the newspapers and the competition between them helps to explain the strength of the union position: it is a relatively easy matter to establish themselves and, once established, to make demands which the managements cannot refuse. The pre-entry labour supply closed shop and the system of payment by task are but two consequences. But this is not entirely without advantages for the managements, since entry into the product market is made that much more difficult. Not only does the would-be competitor have to contend with the costs of capital investment and the competition of well-known brand names, but he cannot expect more favourable terms from the unions.[9] Similarly, no newspaper can gain an advantage over its competitors by exploiting technological change. Secondly, in the absence of effective competition from outside, the managements are able to fix prices and wages — the latter through a form of 'parity' or 'pattern' bargaining — in more or less tacit co-operation with one another;[10] and the fact that there is a system of payment by task means that they can adjust payments and manning levels in the light of changes in demand for the product.

9. It must be pointed out that the situation in Fleet Street is not entirely unique. The argument here follows closely that of H. M. Levinson, *Determining Forces in Collective Wage Bargaining* (New York: J. Wiley, 1966), pp. 264-9. Two other British industries with very similar product market *and* industrial relations characteristics were the docks and exhibition contracting. See, for example, *Final Report of the Committee of Inquiry under the Rt Hon. Lord Devlin into certain matters concerning the Port Transport Industry*, Cmnd. 2734 (London: HMSO, 1965) and NBPI Report No. 117, *Pay and Conditions in the Exhibition Contracting Industry*, Cmnd. 4088 (London: HMSO, 1969). The situation is less extreme in other industries, but here too there is more and more evidence to suggest that the significance of the product market for industrial relations has been neglected far too long. For example, a recent study of piecework bargaining in the engineering industry concludes: 'under relatively full employment and trade union organisation, it is the product market rather than the labour market which has the major impact upon piecework wage determination.' W. Brown, *Piecework Bargaining* (London: Heineman, 1973), p. 175.

10. Again, the situation in Fleet Street is not unique. Writing of the situation in the USA, Hildebrand has suggested that: 'Joint bargaining committees, pattern-following in wage setting, and association bargaining all represent attempts of this kind. In one form or another, these approaches have developed in collective bargaining in the automobile, rubber, basic steel, and construction industries as well as in many others.' G. H. Hildebrand, 'External Influences and the Determination of the Internal Wage Structure', in J. L. Meij (ed.), *Internal Wage-Structure* (Amsterdam: North-Holland, 1963), p. 280.

Finally, it is generally recognized that even substantial reductions in production wages would make little difference to the financial viability of many of the newspapers and so there seems little point in either side trying to effect them. However much they may complain, then, the managements can continue to compete with one another through the columns of the newspapers in the knowledge that no competitor is better or worse off than they are.

Implications for Reform

Only if the proprietors were to combine their manufacturing operations into one printing plant or if a National Publishing Corporation was set up which leased plant to prospective newspaper publishers would the effects of the product market situation described above be overcome. But neither of these events is likely to take place in the short term, if ever. For the foreseeable future, then, any proposals for reform would have to take this situation for granted, as this final section will attempt to show.

Payment System and Pay Structure

On the face of it, the system of payment by task which underpins the subcontracting relationship between the managements and chapels seems to offer little scope for reform. Certainly, it would be unrealistic to contemplate the introduction of incentive-based systems such as measured daywork in other than the composing department where Linotype Operators and Piece Case Hands are already paid by results. There are far too many discontinuities in production and there is no tradition of precise measurement which would be needed to make sure that such systems were effective. Above all, the evidence points to the inevitable conclusion that the managements would be unable to maintain control over such systems. On the other hand, the negotiation of comprehensive agreements with their consolidation of the many components of pay into a single 'comprehensive' or 'equated' weekly rate of pay suggests that the managements and chapels would like more stability than is provided by a system of payment by task. It seems, then, that 'staff status' agreements, with inclusive salaries which formed the basis for holiday, sickness and pension payments, might be the most appropriate direction for reform. Overtime could be compensated for by time off in lieu as in many comprehensive agreements. The salaries could also be adjusted at fixed intervals in the light of changes in working arrangements.

Of even greater significance is the fact that the product market situation encourages pattern bargaining and so has implications for the level at which any payment system is negotiated. It might be thought, for example, that it would be realistic to abandon any form of negotiations between the NPA and the trade unions and to negotiate solely at the office level. After all, this is what seems to be happening at the moment, albeit in a haphazard way. But this would do nothing to alleviate the problems caused by the excessive reliance on comparisons with other offices; and as long as the newspapers compete with one another in the product market there is no reason to believe that these comparisons will cease. It might be *more* realistic, then, to accept that earnings on newspapers which are more or less direct substitutes for each other are going to be very much alike because of the similarities in the levels of activity. In which case it might be possible for the NPA and the trade unions to negotiate inclusive salary levels which covered the different categories of newspaper such as the 'evenings', the 'popular dailies', the 'quality dailies' and so on. There could also be variations in these salary levels depending on differences in page sizes which seems to be the most accepted measure of the level of activity. It would also help if the NPA and the trade unions were to reduce the number of wage categories in the existing structure of industry basic rates and to divide the occupations into some five or six grades.

Manning Levels and Working Practices

The achievement of efficient manning levels and working practices has always appeared high on any programme of reform; and since pattern bargaining affects them no less than the components and levels of pay, it could be argued that the NPA and the trade unions should negotiate standard manning levels and practices to apply throughout Fleet Street. But it has to be recognized that any moves in this direction would have profound implications for job security. Failure to take this into account in the past helps to explain why so little progress has been made. Three groups have to be considered. First, there are the 'regulars' already working in Fleet Street. In theory, the size of the labour force could be reduced substantially over a relatively short period of time without redundancy — because of the age structure of workers in the production and maintenance departments. However, for this to happen there would have to be adequate pension arrangements and a no-replacement agreement, which inevitably involves those members of the printing unions who see Fleet Street as the source of employment *in the future* on account of the long-standing pattern of labour supply. So far the managements in Fleet Street have refused to recognize that they have a commitment to this second group of workers. But this position is unrealistic. Somehow the unions and their members have to be compensated for the loss of job opportunities, otherwise there seems little hope of making progress. One way of doing this might be for the managements in Fleet Street to make a contribution to the unions' pension funds as has been done under similar circumstances in the USA.[11]

The existence of a large number of casual workers in the machine and publishing departments adds to the pressure on jobs and they are the third group which must be taken into account. The first priority is to establish the names of those casuals who were wholly dependent on Fleet Street for their livelihood, because many of those listed on the books of the branches have interests outside Fleet Street and present themselves for work on one or two nights a week only. Like the regular worker, those dependent on Fleet Street for their livelihood would have to be given some form of security. This could be done by allocating them to the newspaper offices as in the docks or they could continue as at present with the guarantee of a lump-sum payment on retirement.

Machinery for Change

Finally, it is difficult to see how any reforms can be contemplated unless there are fundamental changes in institutions as well as attitudes. Indeed, the fact that there have been two attempts already

11. P. T. Hartman, *Collective Bargaining and Productivity* (Berkeley: University of California Press, 1969); and H. Kelber and C. Schlesinger, *Union Printers and Controlled Automation* (New York: Collier-Macmillan, 1967).

in the past ten years to establish new institutions — the Joint Board for the National Newspaper Industry in 1964 and the National Newspaper Steering Group in 1970 — suggests that there is recognition of the need for a permanent industry-wide negotiating body on which all the parties are represented. Arguably there is a similar need at office level where the fragmented bargaining is even more of a problem. But more important still is the need for outside help to overcome the lack of expertise and resources which threatens any attempt at change. In fact, there is a great danger that if they were left to their own devices the parties would be unable — and in some cases unwilling — to make changes. It might be sensible, then, to ask the Conciliation and Arbitration Service to assist in any detailed planning and implementation.

This all suggests that any reform of industrial relations in Fleet Street would be a formidable task. But it is hoped that this study has at least demonstrated that the problems are ones which require practical solutions; that answers will not be found simply by moralizing about the behaviour of the parties. The great pity is that it may already be too late.

Appendix I

The *Daily Mirror* Machine Managers' Dispute

This appendix describes the dispute which began in August 1969, when the Machine Managers (NGA) in the *Daily Mirror* office in London claimed that their differential with the Brake Hands (NATSOPA) had been disturbed.[1] It is a study in detail of one particular dispute about the pay structure, but it also provides an excellent opportunity to illustrate the reactions of the parties on a number of similar occasions.

The ill-feeling between Machine Managers and Brake Hands which is at the root of the dispute has been characteristic of their relationship since the early days of NATSOPA.[2] The PMMTS, a strictly craft society requiring a craft qualification from its members, had been slow to organize the Machine Managers on the rotary presses in Fleet Street, and some had joined NATSOPA. (In fact, Machine Managers at the *News of the World* are to this day members of NATSOPA.) Where it had organized them, however, the PMMTS had never relaxed its policy of restricting job opportunities to its existing members, even though the majority had undergone their apprenticeship in the printing industry on flat-bed machines.[3] This barrier to promotion has always been a thorn in the side of the members of NATSOPA. Unless he works on the *News of the World*, no matter how many years' experience he has, the Brake Hand, the most senior NATSOPA grade, can never become a Machine Manager.[4]

1. The second stage of the dispute took place in May of the following year, when many of the events were repeated.
2. The introduction of the ampersand into the title 'National Society of Operative Printers *and* Assistants' was a direct result of one such dispute.
3. Situations do arise, for example, where the newly recruited Machine Manager has little, if any, experience of working on rotary presses.
4. Outside London there is an arrangement, known as the 50-50 agreement, whereby Brake Hands can be promoted to Machine Manager when vacancies occur.

In the printing industry the Brake Hand's rate is firmly established at 87½% of the Machine Manager's. In Fleet Street this had never been the case. What the differential should be in the *Daily Mirror* office was never made very explicit even at the height of the dispute. The relationship between the industry basic rates of the two occupations was always fluctuating. In 1961, for example, the NPA agreed to increase the rates of Brake Hands by 62½p. Absorptions from the cost of living bonus had also narrowed the percentage differential. If anything, the relationship between the earnings of the two occupations was more confused, as Chapter 3 has shown.

By 1967 the *Daily Mirror* management had negotiated comprehensive agreements with both the NATSOPA Night Machine chapel and the NGA Machine Managers' chapel, both agreements involving a reduction in the number of jobs and a sharing of the savings with the chapels. The effect of these agreements on earnings was as follows: the Machine Managers received £40.589 per week and the Brake Hands £36.313, i.e. 89.5% of the Machine Managers' earnings[5] The Machine Managers seemed prepared to accept this situation. In December 1967, however, the management and the NATSOPA Night Machine chapel negotiated a second stage to the comprehensive agreement which also resulted in a reduction in the number of jobs and a sharing of the savings. The effect of this agreement on earnings was as follows: the Machine Managers, after receiving increases in the cost of living bonus, were earning £40.889 and the Brake Hands £39.496, i.e. 96.6% of the Machine Managers' earnings.[6]

The Machine Managers said they were not prepared to accept this narrowing of the differential, insisting that the Brake Hands should receive no more than 87½% of their earnings. The management replied that there had never been a fixed differential. Furthermore, any narrowing in the differential had come about as a result of productivity bargaining; the Machine Managers, they argued, had only to do what the NATSOPA chapel had done, i.e. enter into a second stage of their comprehensive agreement. Negotiations continued between the management and the Machine Managers

5. Strictly speaking, to arrive at a like-with-like situation a sum amounting to £1.521 should be deducted from the earnings of the Brake Hands in recognition of extra Saturdays worked.
6. Again, allowances have to be made for the extra Saturdays worked by the Brake Hands.

until Easter 1968 when the Machine Managers, their patience exhausted, took matters into their own hands by 'going slow'. The result was that a considerable number of copies of the *Daily Mirror* were lost and it needed the intervention of a national officer of the NGA before a compromise was reached. The earnings of the Machine Managers were increased to £45.0 per week. The Machine Managers, in return, agreed to reduce a small number of jobs: to operate a waste scheme;[7] and to handle more issues of larger-size newspapers. However, it was an uneasy compromise. By persuading the Machine Managers to enter into a second stage of the comprehensive agreement, the management seemed to have won an important victory. But it was a hollow one. By increasing the Machine Managers' earnings to £45.0, they had *de facto* agreed that the Brake Hands should receive approximately 87½% of the Machine Managers' earnings. Worse still, it was recognized to be a 'bad' agreement, giving the Machine Managers a more advantageous share of the savings from the reduction in the number of jobs. Later the Machine Managers were to argue that they had also told the management that they would never again 'sell' jobs to restore the differential.

Now it was the turn of the NATSOPA chapel. It did not escape its attention that the management had been more generous to the Machine Managers. It also had another strong argument: its members too were affected by the waste scheme and the larger-size newspapers. The management, therefore, had no alternative but to enter into yet a third stage of the comprehensive agreement to cover these two items. Negotiations concluded in April 1969, the Brake Hands receiving additional payments along with other members of the chapel.

The relationship between the earnings of the Machine Managers and the Brake Hands was also affected by the increases in the industry basic rates due to take place in September 1969. The industry agreements negotiated individually with the three printing trade unions in 1968 provided for an absorption of 55p. from the cost of living bonus and an increase in the industry basic rates of 3% on 1 September 1968, and an absorption of a further 55p. and increase of 2% on 1 September 1969. The absorptions from the cost of living bonus, totalling £1.10, automatically narrowed the

---

7. A number of the offices operate agreements with chapels in the machine departments in order to reduce the amount of wasted newsprint.

differential between the earnings of the Machine Managers and the Brake Hands. Together with the increases in the industry basic rates, they also exposed the different make-up of earnings, resulting, *pro rata*, in a larger increase for the Brake Hands. The numbers in the two chapels had been kept in strict relationship until 1964, since when some 36% of NATSOPA and 21% of NGA shifts had been reduced by stages one and two of the separate comprehensive agreements; the staff reduction payment, which increases automatically with increases in the industry basic rates, was therefore greater in the case of the Brake Hands. From 1 September 1969 the earnings of the Machine Managers and the Brake Hands were due to become £48.342 and £44.475 respectively — and the differential 91.1%[8] The reactions of the Machine Managers were predictable. They reimposed their 'go-slow', and so began a dispute which was to go on for some three weeks. The developments in the dispute are quickly told. On some nights the *Daily Mirror* lost more than half a million copies as a result of the 'go-slow' and paper-breaks.[9] To bring the dispute to a head, the NPA threatened to dismiss *all* NGA members in Fleet Street. Finally, the General Secretary of the TUC intervened to secure a temporary truce.

A working party was set up and a formula was agreed in the third week of September.[10] The dispute seemed to be over. However, the Machine Managers repudiated the settlement and subsequently persuaded the NGA Executive Council to do the same. The Machine Managers took further industrial action in May 1970 and again Fleet Street was almost brought to a halt. Eventually a compromise was reached which substantially conceded the Machine Managers' case. This was made possible by a softening in the relationship

8. The allowance for the extra Saturday nights worked by the Brake Hands was now £1.571. Also a sum amounting to 50p. should be deducted from the earnings of the Machine Managers because of the difference in sick cover payments.

9. Every time there is a paper-break the presses have to be re-sheeted — which takes time. So an increase in the number of paper-breaks almost invariably accompanies industrial action in the machine department.

10. The formula was as follows: two overseers about to leave would be replaced from the chapel but the chapel members would not themselves be replaced; there would be a re-evaluation of the flexibility, paging, and staff reduction payments in the comprehensive agreement; there would be a re-assessment of the effect of the 2% increase in the industry basic rates; sick cover would be extended in the winter period; a new method of adjusting colour would be adopted; night Machine Managers would receive an increase of £1.20 and day Machine Managers an increase of 96p; the question of differentials would form part of the agenda of the proposed joint meeting to discuss the pay structure.

between the NGA and NATSOPA who let it be known that it would not in effect veto any agreement reached at the *Daily Mirror*; there was also an indication that the two chapels would negotiate jointly with the management if the initial grievance was removed. Once this position became known, there was a waning of support among other members of the NPA.

The positions of the parties may be summed up as follows. The Machine Managers argued throughout that the differential should be restored to what it had been at Easter 1968. They were not prepared to enter into the third stage of the comprehensive agreement, arguing that they had made the management well aware of this in 1968. One justification for this position was the uncertainty surrounding the future of the *Sun*; if the *Sun* should close, they argued, they would need the jobs to absorb any redundancies. But their opposition to what many members of the NGA termed 'job selling' was much deeper. The FOC, an influential figure in the London Region of the NGA, never wavered from the view, sometimes expressed in highly emotional terms, that there would be no end to this process. It was an article of faith among Machine Managers in Fleet Street, totally unjustified in the case of the *Daily Mirror*, that the 'NATSOPAs' had more jobs to 'sell'; that a position would be reached where the differential would in fact be reversed. The Machine Managers at the *Daily Mirror*, therefore, were carrying the banner for members of the NGA in other offices.

This also explains why the Machine Managers at the *Daily Mirror* had the unfailing support of the officers of the London Region of the NGA, which eventually was to swing the full weight of the Executive Council behind them. The position of the national officers was somewhat different. At first they supported the Machine Managers, arguing that a simple compromise, similar to that negotiated at Easter 1968, was all that was necessary. When it became obvious that the management's hands were tied, they investigated the possibility of negotiating an agreement involving a reduction in the number of jobs. When they found that the Machine Managers were not prepared to take advice from anyone, the issue became one of discipline. Finally, they were forced to put their weight behind the Machine Managers, once the Executive Council had been persuaded to support them; only the threat of dismissal brought the national officers back to the negotiating table.

The management were in an unenviable position. They had

179

committed the unpardonable sin in Fleet Street of allowing the two sets of negotiations to get out of hand. Once this had happened, they were in difficulties. If they made concessions to the Machine Managers, the NATSOPA chapel would inevitably apply pressure. They wanted to negotiate with the two chapels jointly, but neither would agree. Moreover, there was an important principle at stake. The *Daily Mirror* had pioneered the idea of comprehensive agreements involving a reduction in the number of jobs, believing this to be the only way of improving the efficiency of production in Fleet Street; if they once admitted that the Machine Managers, whose number had been kept in strict ratio with those of NATSOPA members, should receive an increase in earnings unrelated to improvements in productivity, then any hope of persuading other chapels to do this would be lost.

This principle also helps to explain why the other members of NPA supported the management at the *Daily Mirror*. There was criticism of their handling of the negotiations, but an underlying sympathy with the position in which the *Daily Mirror* management found themselves. Furthermore, at the height of the dispute they found that they were as helpless as the management at the *Daily Mirror*: the Executive Council of NATSOPA informed the NPA that if any concessions were made to the Machine Managers, NATSOPA chapels throughout Fleet Street would be instructed to demand the staffing levels in force before the negotiation of comprehensive agreements. The NPA's problem was to find some way of expressing more than moral support for the *Daily Mirror* — hence the threat to dismiss all members of the NGA in Fleet Street. In effect, it has been argued, this is the only sanction available to the NPA which also protects the newspaper suffering industrial action from the competition of other newspapers. If workers can be denied earnings, even for a short time, they might be deterred. Attitudes changed once NATSOPA let it be known that it would not stand in the way of an agreement. Inevitably self-interest prevailed. There was more and more criticism of the handling of the negotiations, and a waning of support for any further resistance.

The *Daily Mirror* Machine Managers' dispute illustrates many of the characteristics of industrial relations in Fleet Street. The fragmented nature of the negotiations between the managements and chapels, the intensity of feeling with which differentials are protected, and the inherent weakness of the managements and the NPA when faced by localized industrial action — all these deserve special emphasis.

The SLADE Dispute, 1968

In August 1967 the NPA anticipated the ending of the 1964 industry agreements, asking for the trade unions' co-operation in overcoming the industry's problems which had been intensified by devaluation. The industry, the unions were told, could not afford an increase in its labour costs; there could be no straightforward increases in the industry basic rates, plus a cost of living bonus and a long-term agreement.

The trade unions asked for an opportunity to consider what the NPA had said, and replied to the NPA's proposals in November. They said that their members were expecting an increase in earnings but were not opposed to discussing ways and means of doing this within the constraints imposed by the NPA. The NPA confirmed that there could be no increase in earnings without measured increases in the industry's productivity. It agreed, however, to continue the cost of living bonus pending further discussions with the trade unions.

As a result, it was agreed to set up a working party comprising members of the Labour Executive and the general secretaries who would decide matters of general principle such as the allocation of the savings from productivity bargaining. The NPA would also meet with individual branches in an endeavour to clear away any obstacles to the negotiations which the NPA hoped would take place between the managements and chapels.

The working party discussions carried on in a desultory fashion until May 1968, the trade unions enjoying the benefit of increases in the cost of living bonus. In May, however, SOGAT (Divisions 1 and A) withdrew from the discussions; relationships between SOGAT and the NGA had reached their worst and the two unions were hardly talking to each other.

The NPA decided it must now bring matters to a head, and

announced that there would be no further increases in the cost of living bonus from 1 June 1968. This quickly brought the trade unions to the negotiating table, albeit singly. Negotiations between the NPA and SOGAT and the NGA were completed successfully on identical terms: a package agreement involving absorption from the cost of living bonus and increases in the industry basic rates in September 1968 and 1969, and guide-lines for productivity bargaining between the managements and chapels. SLADE, however, refused to accept these terms. It strongly resented the unilateral ending of the cost of living bonus. It was also violently opposed to a reference to method study which was contained in the proposed guide-lines for productivity bargaining. There were 'go-slows' in a number of the offices beginning in the first week of July.

The 'go-slows' proved irksome to the managements but did not prevent them from producing a newspaper. Moreover, many newspapers were able to cope by using so-called 'stock blocks' of standard photographs which are kept on file. Once the NPA looked like settling with the NGA and SOGAT, SLADE had no hope of success. On 2 August the NPA warned that unless there was a guarantee of normal working in all offices SLADE members who had been taking industrial action would be summarily dismissed at 6 p.m. the following Monday, 5 August. The guarantees were not given and the managements duly dismissed their SLADE employees. The lock-out lasted some six weeks, SLADE eventually accepting the same terms as the NGA and SOGAT.

The SLADE dispute illustrates the difficulties with which the NPA and the trade unions were faced in negotiating revisions to the industry basic rates. Of course, the NPA's position in this particular dispute was much stronger for the fact that SLADE is the only trade union with members in Fleet Street who are unable to stop production totally.

The SOGAT Dispute, 1970

The NPA also took the initiative in the events which led up to the SOGAT dispute in 1970, asking for a meeting with the trade unions in April 1970 to discuss the ending of the industry agreement in August. The theme was much the same as in 1967: the NPA wanted to discuss ways and means of improving the efficiency of production. This time, however, the emphasis was on sorting out the problems of the pay structure through negotiations between the NPA and the trade unions collectively, a subject to the fore of attention because of the *Daily Mirror* Machine Managers' dispute described in Appendix I.

The trade unions were non-commital. A few weeks later, however, SOGAT (Divisions 1 and A) and SLADE submitted a claim for an interim increase in the industry basic rates of 25%. (In fact, the two Divisions of SOGAT had originally submitted different claims, Division 1 for 20% and Division A for 25%.) The two unions justified their claims on the grounds of increases in the cost of living and increases in other industries. Furthermore, they argued, there were to be no 'strings attached'.

The NPA were placed in an awkward position. They wanted to negotiate with the trade unions collectively, preferably with the maintenance unions included. On the other hand, it did not seem possible to refuse to discuss the claim submitted by the two unions. Matters came to a head at a meeting on Friday 26 May. The NPA listened to the arguments delivered in support of the claim and then replied that it wanted to negotiate with the trade unions collectively. Whereupon the two unions became incensed, the officials of SOGAT (Division 1), in particular, threatening strike action the following Tuesday unless the NPA altered its position.

The NPA decided that it could not accede to the claims. They were totally unrealistic, it was argued, and would lead to repercussive claims from the NGA. As it happened, SOGAT had made no preparations for a strike, believing that the NPA was sure to back down. When it did not, SOGAT was forced to carry out its threat.

So began negotiations which the general secretary of the TUC is reputed to have described as 'the toughest, most complicated, and complex I've ever seen in all my life'.[1] Many hours were spent at Congress House and 10 Downing Street where the Prime Minister, anxious that the public should not be deprived of newspapers during the run-up to the forthcoming election, was often an active participant.

Once SOGAT was on strike, the NPA decided that there was no alternative but to insist on a settlement involving all the unions. In fact, this was the major issue of the negotiations. At first the NGA and the maintenance unions were reluctant to become involved. Finally, the NGA was persuaded to join the negotiations on condition that there was an increase in the industry basic rates. The agreement, to which all the production and maintenance unions were party, provided for an increase in these rates of 5% with effect from 1 July, or a cash sum equivalent to 10% of the industry basic rate, whichever was the larger; an extra week's holiday; and the setting up of a working party (the National Newspaper Steering Group) to examine the pay structure and manpower situation. The strike ended late on Friday 2 June.

The SOGAT dispute, like the SLADE dispute, illustrates the difficulties with which the NPA and the trade unions were faced in negotiating revisions to the industry basic rates. More significantly, the SOGAT dispute demonstrates the lengths to which the NPA felt compelled to go in order to avoid treating any one union more favourably than the others.

1. The *Sunday Times*, 4 June 1970.